HLSL and Pixel Shaders for XAML Developers

Walt Ritscher

O'REILLY®

Beijing · Cambridge · Farnham · Köln · Sebastopol · Tokyo

HLSL and Pixel Shaders for XAML Developers
by Walt Ritscher

Published by O'Reilly Media, Inc., 1005 Gravenstein Highway North, Sebastopol, CA 95472.

O'Reilly books may be purchased for educational, business, or sales promotional use. Online editions are also available for most titles (*http://my.safaribooksonline.com*). For more information, contact our corporate/institutional sales department: 800-998-9938 or *corporate@oreilly.com*.

Editor: Rachel Roumeliotis   **Cover Designer:** Karen Montgomery
Production Editor: Rachel Steely   **Interior Designer:** David Futato
Proofreader: Rachel Steely   **Illustrators:** Robert Romano and Rebecca Demarest

Revision History for the First Edition:
    2012-07-03   First release
See *http://oreilly.com/catalog/errata.csp?isbn=9781449319847* for release details.

ISBN: 978-1-449-31984-7

[LSI]

1341331317

Table of Contents

Preface

Pixel Shaders are one of the more powerful graphic tools available for XAML programmers. I first encountered them in the Windows Presentation Foundation 3.5 SP1 release and was completely smitten. It didn't take long to learn that I could create custom shaders, commonly called Effects in WPF, and add them to my projects. Excited by the prospect, I started my research and soon learned that shaders are written in a language called High Level Shader Language (HLSL). I like programming challenges and learning new technologies, so I set off to learn more about custom shaders. I downloaded the DirectX SDK, opened the documentation, and started digging through the pages.

It was at this point that I ran into the wall of uncertainty.

Shader development is very different from working in XAML element trees, and bears little resemblance to traditional .NET programming. The overall mindset is different: the language looks similar to C but uses a quaint semantic syntax and the documentation is sparse and confusing. I found myself writing shader code and hesitantly testing the output, never quite sure what would show up onscreen.

I learned later that I'm not alone in feeling unsure when writing HLSL algorithms. I talked to countless Silverlight developers who echoed my feelings of doubt when faced with the prospect of writing custom shaders. I was reassured to learn, while attending a daylong game workshop, that many game development shops have dedicated shader developers who specialize in mastering this arcane craft. The reason is clear: it takes a different mindset to understand shaders and some developers are better suited to the skills needed to write successful effects.

As a result, I started designing tools and tutorials to simplify the shader learning process for XAML developers. I didn't know it at the time, but that road was to lead me to O'Reilly and the writing of this book.

Who This Book Is For

This book is aimed squarely at the Silverlight, WPF, and XAML developer crowd. It's meant to be a reliable introduction to the eccentric world of GPU programming. I assume that you are familiar with .NET and have passing knowledge of XAML. I'm not teaching programming or XAML, so having some measure of programming experience is essential before you read this book. For this book, I'll use C# for the .NET code but all examples are easily translated to Visual Basic.

No previous Direct3D or HLSL knowledge is required.

What You Need to Use This Book

For developing custom shaders, you need only a text editor and an HLSL compiler. The compiler is included in the DirectX SDK, which is available at *http://msdn.microsoft .com/directx/*. To build a .NET wrapper for the custom shader, it's convenient to use Visual Studio 2010 and .NET 4.0. Expression Blend 4 provides a delightful designer tool that makes it easy to drag shaders onto your UI elements and preview the results in real time.

I've written a free utility called Shazzam Shader Editor, which greatly simplifies writing, compiling, and testing shaders. I use Shazzam extensively throughout this book and I encourage you to download a copy from *http://shazzam-tool.com* and follow along with the book examples. If you install Shazzam, you don't need to install the massive DirectX SDK. Furthermore, Shazzam contains all the sample shaders discussed in this book.

Contents of This Book

Here is what each chapter of the book will cover.

Chapter 1: This chapter introduces the basics of shader programming, including a look into the early history of 3D programming.

Chapter 2: The first exploratory steps to creating a XAML specific shader are investigated in this chapter. It provides a quick tour of the shader features covered in the following chapters.

Chapter 3: There are a bewildering number of shader types available to the effect developer. This chapter highlights the common shader types, breaking them down into sensible categories.

Chapter 4: This chapter examines in detail the working parts of the XAML Shader Effect class. It shows how the HLSL and XAML code work in conjunction to create effects that utilize the power of XAML applications.

Chapter 5: Visual Studio and Expression Blend are the premium Microsoft developer and designer tools. This chapter explores the shader specific tools available in these powerful IDEs.

Chapter 6: Shazzam is a free standalone shader editor that contains all the tools you need to compile, test, and visualize your custom pixel shaders. This chapter shows how to use this interesting tool.

Chapter 7: Writing a shader effect requires learning the HLSL programming language. This chapter tours the important features and syntax rules of this quirky DirectX dialect.

Chapter 8: This chapter tours a broad range of topics, gleaned from real world effect development, and shows how to take the knowledge from the previous chapters and write effective shaders.

Appendix A: A list of resources for learning more about pixel shader development.

Appendix B: A reference appendix containing descriptions of the Shazzam shader tags.

Conventions Used in This Book

The following typographical conventions are used in this book:

Plain text
> Indicates menu titles, menu options, menu buttons, and keyboard accelerators (such as Alt and Ctrl).

Italic
> Indicates new terms, URLs, email addresses, filenames, file extensions, pathnames, directories, and Unix utilities.

`Constant width`
> Indicates commands, options, switches, variables, attributes, keys, functions, types, classes, namespaces, methods, modules, properties, parameters, values, objects, events, event handlers, XML tags, HTML tags, macros, the contents of files, or the output from commands.

`Constant width bold`
> Shows commands or other text that should be typed literally by the user.

`Constant width italic`
> Shows text that should be replaced with user-supplied values.

 This icon signifies a tip, suggestion, or general note.

 This icon indicates a warning or caution.

Using Code Examples

This book is here to help you get your job done. In general, you may use the code in this book in your programs and documentation. You do not need to contact us for permission unless you're reproducing a significant portion of the code. For example, writing a program that uses several chunks of code from this book does not require permission. Selling or distributing a CD-ROM of examples from O'Reilly books does require permission. Answering a question by citing this book and quoting example code does not require permission. Incorporating a significant amount of example code from this book into your product's documentation does require permission.

We appreciate, but do not require, attribution. An attribution usually includes the title, author, publisher, and ISBN. For example: "*HLSL and Pixel Shaders for XAML Developers* by Walt Ritscher (O'Reilly). Copyright 2011 Walt Ritscher, 978-1-449-31984-7."

If you feel your use of code examples falls outside fair use or the permission given above, feel free to contact us at *permissions@oreilly.com*.

Safari® Books Online

Safari Books Online (*www.safaribooksonline.com*) is an on-demand digital library that delivers expert content in both book and video form from the world's leading authors in technology and business.

Technology professionals, software developers, web designers, and business and creative professionals use Safari Books Online as their primary resource for research, problem solving, learning, and certification training.

Safari Books Online offers a range of product mixes and pricing programs for organizations, government agencies, and individuals. Subscribers have access to thousands of books, training videos, and prepublication manuscripts in one fully searchable database from publishers like O'Reilly Media, Prentice Hall Professional, Addison-Wesley Professional, Microsoft Press, Sams, Que, Peachpit Press, Focal Press, Cisco Press, John Wiley & Sons, Syngress, Morgan Kaufmann, IBM Redbooks, Packt, Adobe Press, FT Press, Apress, Manning, New Riders, McGraw-Hill, Jones & Bartlett, Course Technology, and dozens more. For more information about Safari Books Online, please visit us online.

How to Contact Us

Please address comments and questions concerning this book to the publisher:

O'Reilly Media, Inc.
1005 Gravenstein Highway North
Sebastopol, CA 95472
800-998-9938 (in the United States or Canada)
707-829-0515 (international or local)
707-829-0104 (fax)

We have a web page for this book, where we list errata, examples, and any additional information. You can access this page at:

> *http://oreil.ly/hlsl_px_shaders*

To comment or ask technical questions about this book, send email to:

> *bookquestions@oreilly.com*

For more information about our books, courses, conferences, and news, see our website at *http://www.oreilly.com*.

Find us on Facebook: *http://facebook.com/oreilly*

Follow us on Twitter: *http://twitter.com/oreillymedia*

Watch us on YouTube: *http://www.youtube.com/oreillymedia*

Acknowledgments

No author can complete a book without the help of other people. I'd like to thank:

- The O'Reilly Media Team: The publishing industry is changing rapidly; the disruptive vortex known as the Internet is relentlessly crushing the old print empires. O'Reilly seems undaunted by the sinkholes opening in their neighborhood; they keep finding innovative ways to stay relevant. A book like mine, small in pagecount, targeting a niche topic, would never have been published five years ago. However, O'Reilly is embracing the eBook market and rethinking what it means to publish a book in this era. Thanks for inviting me to the O'Reilly author circle.

- My editor, Rachel Roumeliotis, gets kudos for listening to my original book pitch and advocating the project within the shadowy walls of the O'Reilly castle. Little did she know that once we had the green light she'd get an endless stream of email queries as I learned the idiosyncrasies of the O'Reilly book production process. Rachel, the next book will be done sooner, I promise!

- I knew that finding a tech reviewer for this project would be a challenge. The number of XAML experts that also know HLSL is a very short list. René Schulte (*http://kodierer.blogspot.com/*) is one of that elite crew and he signed on as tech editor the moment he heard about the project. He's a busy guy, a productive writer in his own right, and he has an impressive list of Silverlight and phone applications to his credit. But that didn't stop him from offering pointed criticism when it was needed. This could easily have been his book: his knowledge of computer vision, bitmaps, shaders, and the entire pixel pipeline is top-notch. Thanks for keeping me on track, René.

- The Review team. Jeremiah Morrill read an early draft of the first chapter. His enthusiastic comments were a huge motivation for me to finish the book. David Kelley reviewed the first half of the book and immediately replied with constructive feedback. Thanks to both of you, for helping me see my manuscript with fresh eyes.

- My wife, Amy, is a writer. She finished two drafts of her novel (eighty thousand words!) while I slowly worked my way to the conclusion of this techie novella. She did this while ferrying our daughter to endless vocal rehearsals and play practices. We had many discussions about writing; during the production of this book, she was always ready to listen to my writing questions and offer constructive advice. Amy, you are a truly one of a kind, a real jewel!

- I'm grateful to the following photographers for releasing their beautiful images with a creative commons license: Richard Taylor, Mike Keeling, and SolStock.

- Cory Plotts graciously submitted his Photoshop blend mode shaders to the project. You can learn more about them at his blog (*http://www.cplotts.com/2009/06/16/ blend-modes-part-i/*).

- I'm sure many readers are familiar with Pete Brown (*http://10rem.net*). He's highly visible to the XAML community, constantly sharing his UI and XAML knowledge with the world. Pete is also a successful book author. My advice: buy anything he writes. His books are full of useful information, his prose laced with humorous asides and geek-related commentary. I am thrilled to have Pete write the forward to this book.

- Finally, I'd like to thank my readers. You were always at the back of my mind, as I wrestled with the best way to explain the HLSL technology in each chapter.

Foreword

As developers, we often find ourselves in a position where we need to learn a new programming or markup language in order to support our primary development tasks. Desktop programmers end up learning XML and XSLT. Web programmers find SQL is a necessary part of their skillset. C programmers on microcontrollers find they really need some inline assembly for a critical section of code. HTML/JS tends to be one of those skills everyone is expected to have. And yes, Silverlight, WPF, XNA, and C++ developers find they must write HLSL to provide just the right effect at the maximum possible performance. The day of the one-trick pony is rapidly coming to an end.

Typically, these languages augment our applications; they help get us past roadblocks, and perhaps most importantly, they present a different way to think about programming. It's this last point I consider the most important: polyglot programmers are the ones who tend to come up with the best solutions to problems, because they have a larger universe of possible ideas, approaches, and algorithms to choose from.

HLSL is different enough from our regular workhorse-language programming that we can't help but learn some new techniques from it. Instead of explicit loops in a function, the algorithms work with individual pixels or vertices with code which is being called millions of times under external control. Instead of being spun through on a single thread on the CPU, or a well-behaved foreground/background thread pair, you're looking at code which is being run in a massively parallel configuration on a video card's GPU with hundreds or even thousands of concurrent instances. For many, this will be their first taste of writing truly parallel code.

Initially, an entire book just on HLSL may seem odd. Once you get into it, however, you realize just how deep and rich and complex a topic this is. The HLSL shader is as fundamental a part of graphics manipulation as the `for` loop or `function` call is in procedural code. Not only are you learning something new and interesting that will contribute to your overall knowledge, but you're learning a key skill that will open doors for far more interesting applications than the yet-another-forms-over-data app you probably have on your plate.

That's not to say shaders are useful only for their educational properties. Quite the contrary! Once you understand how they work, and how to code them, you'll find that you can implement all sorts of interesting visuals, from subtle animations in a user interface to image manipulation. If it involves coloring a pixel, a shader can almost certainly do it. Best of all, once you figure out how to do it, you'll be able to use the shader in Silverlight, WPF, XNA, C++, and more.

When learning pixel manipulation using shaders, you're learning the right tool for the job. If you use the wrong tool, the implications can be disastrous, especially when it comes to performance. Just ask the WPF team about bitmap effects the next time you have one of them cornered. It seemed to make sense at the time, but performance was...lacking. They've since been deprecated in favor of shader-based effects.

I've known Walt for a number of years through our joint work in the XAML community, both before and after I joined Microsoft. His passion around XAML and .NET, as well as his knowledge of shaders, design, and graphics uniquely qualifies him to write a book like this. I knew what to expect when I read the early copy, and I wasn't disappointed. I mean, this is the guy who wrote Shazzam! Oh, and naming a product "Shazzam"? Awesome. We should hire him to help out in our own product names at Microsoft.

Walt excels in presenting a complex subject in such a way that any developer can understand it. He doesn't just skim the surface (something I am very guilty of when I wrote about shaders in Silverlight), but rather explores all the dark corners to provide much needed insight—both technical and historical. It's rare to find an author who can do that on a complex subject like this, and then simultaneously cover two similar but different platforms like Silverlight and WPF.

The combination of XAML with C# or VB makes for a powerful platform for user interface design and development. There is always something new and interesting you can do. In Windows 8, we've expanded XAML so you can use your skills (and reuse your markup) in C++. The time you spend working in XAML is time well spent. It's a skill you can carry forward with confidence.

I'm proud to work with Walt because of his passion for XAML, his ability to educate others, and his ongoing support for the community.

I'm also happy to work with the Silverlight, WPF, and Windows Metro XAML teams at Microsoft. They are dedicated to the products and customers, and passionate about what they do. While humble, they know they are delivering something useful and interesting; something which has a long future in front of it; something which gets developers and designers excited. I'm excited to see Walt once again sharing his knowledge, expertise, and passion about these technologies in what has turned out to be an essential addition to any XAML designer or developer's library.

—Pete Brown
XAML and Blinking LED Gadget Guy, Microsoft

CHAPTER 1

Shader 101

It seems an obvious question to ask at the beginning of an *HLSL* and shader book; what exactly is a shader? It's a small program or algorithm written explicitly to run on a computer Graphics Processing Unit (*GPU*). It provides a way for developers to extend the rendering capabilities of the GPU. Any program that works closely with graphics will benefit from using shaders. The video game industry spins off custom shaders by the thousands; they are as vital to game projects as business entity classes are to line-of-business (LOB) applications. Nothing prohibits business programmers from experimenting with shaders in their LOB applications; in fact, recent trends in user interface (UI) design and information visualization cry out for shader use.

Because shaders run at the kernel level of the GPU, they are automatically parallelized by the GPU hardware and are extremely fast at manipulating graphic output. Typically, the GPU can process shaders several orders of magnitude faster than if the shader code is run on a CPU.

Why Should XAML Developers Learn HLSL?

If you are an *XAML* developer, I'll wager you've heard about pixel shaders. In fact, you may be using some of these effects in your application already. WPF introduced the *DropShadowEffect* and *BlurEffect* in .NET 3.5 SP1 and both of these classes take advantage of pixel shaders. *Silverlight* added pixel shaders in Silverlight 3. The Windows Phone team disappointed developers by dropping support for shaders before the final release of their hardware. Microsoft had good reason to ditch phone shaders, as they caused a significant drag on performance, but their loss is still lamentable. To make up for that setback, the Silverlight 5 release includes support for XNA models and shaders.

This is awesome news, as it means that you can mix XNA and Silverlight 5 together in the same application and that gives you access to another essential shader type: the *Vertex* shader.

XNA is a Microsoft framework that facilitates game development on the PC, the Xbox 360, and Windows Phone 7. It give you access to the power of DirectX without having to leave the comfort of your favorite .NET programming languages. To learn more about XNA, get a copy of Learning XNA 4.0 by Aaron Reed from: *http://shop.oreilly.com/product/0636920013709.do*

As an XAML developer, do you need to write your own shaders? No, not really; you may spend your entire career without ever using a shader. Even if you use a shader, you may never have the need to write your own, as there are free shader effects included in Microsoft Expression Blend and also in the .NET framework. While it's nice to have these prebuilt effects, they represent only a fraction of the possibilities discovered by graphics programmers. Microsoft is not in the shader business, at least not directly. A core part of their business is building flexible programming languages and frameworks. The *DirectX* team follows this path and provides several shader programming languages for custom development. So if you have an idea for an interesting effect or want to modify an existing effect, you'll need to write a custom shader. When you cross that threshold and decide to build a custom shader, you have some learning ahead of you. You need to learn a new programming language called HLSL.

I've started using the term XAML development in the last year. Extensible Application Markup Language (XAML) is the core markup for Windows Presentation Foundation, Microsoft Surface, Silverlight, and Windows Phone applications. There are differences among these technologies, but they all share a common markup in XAML. Even the new Metro application framework for Windows 8 uses XAML as its primary markup implementation. I find that WPF and Silverlight developers have more in common with one another than they have differences. Since there is so much overlap in skills between these XAML-based systems, I think XAML developer is a suitable umbrella term that symbolizes this commonality.

The Tale of the Shader

To understand the history behind shaders, we need to go back a few decades and look inside the mind of George Lucas. Thirty years ago, George had produced the first movies in his highly successful *Star Wars* series. These first movies relied on using miniaturized models and special camera rigs to generate the futuristic effects. Lucas could already see the limitations of this camera-based system and he figured that generating his models in software would be a better approach. Therefore, he established a software division at LucasFilm and hired a team of smart people to build a graphics rendering system. Eventually the software division he created was sold off and became Pixar.

The engineers hired by Lucas took their responsibilities seriously and were soon generating 3D objects within software. But these computer-generated models failed when spliced into the live action, as they suffered from a lack of realism. The problem is that a raw 3D object looks stark and unnatural to the movie viewer, and won't blend with the rest of the movie scene. In other words, it will be painfully obvious that there is a computer-generated item up on the big screen. In the quest to solve this problem, an engineer named Rob Cook decided to write a 'shading' processor to help make the items look more realistic. His idea was to have software analyze the 3D object and the surrounding scene and determine where the shadows fell and light reflected onto the model. Then the shader engine could modify the film output to imitate the real world placement of the artificial artifact. To be fair, there were existing shade tools available, but they were primitive and inflexible. Rob's breakthrough idea was to make a scriptable pipeline of graphic operations. These operations were customizable and easy to string together to create a complex effect. These "shaders" eventually became part of an infamous graphics program called Renderman, which remains the primary rendering tool used for every Pixar movie. While you may not be familiar with the Renderman name, you certainly have seen the output from this phenomenal program in movies like *Toy Story 3*.

Pixar has an informative section devoted to Renderman on their website at *http://ren derman.pixar.com/products/index/renderman.html*.

The beginnings of this shader revolution started back in the early 1980s and ran on specialized hardware. But the computer industry is never idle. By the late nineties, 3D graphics accelerator cards started to show up in high-end PCs. It wasn't long before card manufacturers figured out how to combine 2D and 3D circuits into a single chip and the modern Graphics Processor Unit (GPU) was born. At this same time, the GPU manufacturers came up with their own innovative idea—real-time rendering—which allows processing of 3D scenes while the application is running. Prior to this breakthrough, the rendering was performed offline. The burgeoning game development industry embraced this graphics advance with enthusiasm and soon 3D frameworks like *OpenGL* and Microsoft *Direct3D* were attracting followers. This is the point in the story where HLSL enters the picture.

HLSL and DirectX

In the early days of GPUs, the 3D features were implemented as embedded code within the video card chips. These Fixed Functions, as they were known, were not very customizable and so chipmakers added new features by retooling the chips and throwing hardware at the problem. At some point, Microsoft decided this was solvable with software and devised an assembly language approach to address the problem. This worked and made custom shaders possible, but required developers who could work in assembly language. Assembly language is notoriously complex and hard to read. For example, here is a small sample of shader assembly code for your reading pleasure (Example 1-1).

Example 1-1. Shader written in Assembly Language

```
; A simple pixel shader
; Use the ps 2.0 instruction set and registers
ps_2_0
;
; Declare a sampler for the s0 register
dcl_2d s0
; Declare t0 to use 2D texture coordinates
dcl t0.xy
; sample the texture into the r1 register
texld r1, t0, s0
; move r1 to the output register
mov oC0, r1
```

 DirectX 8.0 was the first version to include programmable shaders. It first appeared in 2000 and included the assembly level APIs.

Working in assembly takes a special breed of programmer and they are in short supply. NVidia and Microsoft saw this as an opportunity to bolster the PC graphics market and collaborated to create a more accessible shader language. NVidia named their language *Cg* while Microsoft chose the name *High Level Shader Language* (HLSL) for their version. Cg and HLSL have virtually identical syntax; they are branded differently for each company. Both languages compile shaders for DirectX. Cg has the additional benefit of compiling shaders for the OpenGL framework.

 The Open Graphics Library, a.k.a. OpenGL, is an open source, cross-platform 2D/3D graphics API.

These higher level languages are based on the C language (in fact the name Cg stands for *C for Graphics*) and use curly brackets, semicolons, and other familiar C styled syntax. HLSL also brings high-level concepts like functions, expressions, named variables, and statements to the shader programmer. HLSL debuted in DirectX 9.0 in 2002 and has seen steady updates since its release.

Let's contrast the assembly language shown in Example 1-1 with the equivalent code in HLSL (Example 1-2).

Example 1-2. Shader written in HLSL

```
sampler2D ourImage;

float4 main(float2 locationInSource : TEXCOORD) : COLOR
{
  return tex2D( ourImage , locationInSource.xy);
}
```

Here, the first line is declaring a variable name `ourImage`, which is the input into the shader. The next line defines a function called `main` that takes a single parameter and returns a value. That return value is vital, as it is the output of the pixel shader. That "float4" represents the RGBA values that are assigned to the pixel shown on the screen.

This is about the simplest pixel shader imaginable. Trust me, there are more details ahead. This is a preliminary look at shader code; there are detailed discussions of HLSL syntax throughout the remainder of this book.

 This is the first HLSL example in the book but it should be obvious to anyone with a modicum of programming experience that the HLSL version is easier to read and understand than the assembly language version.

Understanding the Graphics Pipeline

HLSL is the shader programming language for Direct3D, which is a part of Microsoft's DirectX API. Appendix A contains a detailed account of Direct3D and the graphics-programming pipeline. What follows is a simplified account of the important parts of the shader workflow.

To understand pixel shaders in the XAML world requires a quick look at how they work in their original Direct3D world. Building a 3D object starts with defining a model. In DirectX, a model (a.k.a. *mesh*) is a mathematical representation of a 3D object. These meshes are defined as arrays of vertices. This vertex map becomes the initial input into the rendering pipeline.

 If you studied geometry, you've seen the term vertex. In solid geometry, a vertex represents a point where three planes meet.

In the DirectX realm, a vertex is more than a 3D point, however. It represents a 3D location, so it must have x, y, and z coordinate information. Vertices may also be defined with color, texture, and lighting characteristics.

The 3D model is not viewable on screen without conversion. Currently the two most popular conversion techniques are ray tracing and rasterization. Rasterization is widespread on modern GPUs because it is fast, which enables high frame rates—a must for computer games.

As I mentioned before, the DirectX graphics pipeline is complex, but for illustration purposes, I'll whittle it down to these few components (Figure 1-1.)

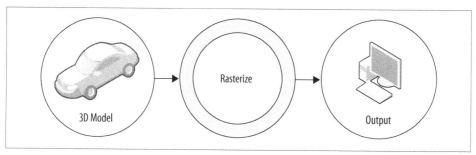

Figure 1-1. Three DirectX pipeline components

DirectX injects two other important components into this pipeline. Between the model and the rasterizer lives the vertex shader (Figure 1-2). Vertex shaders are algorithms that transform the vertex information stored in the model before handoff to the rasterizer.

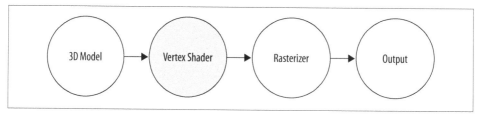

Figure 1-2. The vertex shader in the pipeline

Vertex shaders get the first opportunity to change the initial model. Vertex Shaders simply change the values of the data, so that a vertex emerges with a different texture, different color, or a different position in space. Vertex shaders are a popular way to distort the original shape and are used to apply the first lighting pass to the object. The output of this stage is passed to the rasterizer. At this point in the pipeline, the rasterized data is ready for the computer display. This is where the pixel shader, if there is one, goes to work.

The pixel shader examines each rasterized pixel (Figure 1-3), applies the shader algorithm, and outputs the final color value. They are frequently used to blend additional textures with the original raster image. They excel at color modification and image distortion. If you want to apply a subtle leather texture to an image, the pixel shader is your tool.

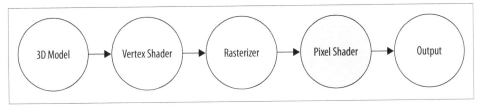

Figure 1-3. The pixel shader in the pipeline

XAML and Shaders

Now that you've learned the fundamentals of the DirectX pipeline, you're ready to take a closer look at how Silverlight and WPF use shaders. Let's examine what happens in the WPF world first. In WPF, the underlying graphics engine is DirectX. That means that even on a simple business form consisting of a few text controls, the screen output travels through the DirectX pipeline (the very same pipeline described above). WPF takes your XAML UI tree and works its magic on it, instantiating the elements, configuring bindings, and performing other essential tasks. Once it has the UI ready, it passes it off to DirectX which rasterizes the image as described earlier. Here's what the process looked like in the first release of WPF (Figure 1-4).

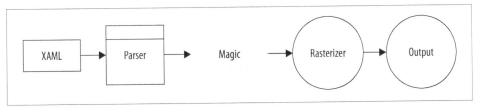

Figure 1-4. WPF 3.0 render process

As you can see, there were no vertex or pixel shaders available. It took another couple years for Microsoft to add shaders to the mix. Pixel shaders appeared in .NET 3.5 in 2007 and now the process looks like this (Figure 1-5).

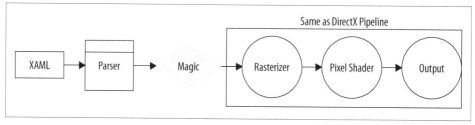

Figure 1-5. WPF 3.5 adds pixel shaders to the render process

Notice how the end of this pipeline is identical to the 3D model pipeline cited earlier. As you can see, the input data for a pixel shader is the output from the rasterizer. It really doesn't matter to the shader whether that information is a rasterized version of a complex 3D shape or the output from an XAML visual tree. The shader works the same way for both, since it is only 2D information at this point.

You might notice that there are no Vertex shaders in the WPF pipeline. That's not an omission on my part. Vertex shaders are not available to WPF and there are no plans to add them to WPF. The likely reason for this oversight was the release of XNA, Microsoft's managed game development platform. XNA has a tight relationship with DirectX/Direct3D and treats 3D and models nearly the same as native DirectX.

Don't be too sad over the loss of the vertex shader—pixel shaders are still a powerful technique and can create a variety of useful effects. In fact, since current PC hardware is so powerful, game developers often prefer using pixel shaders for lighting calculations, a job that used to be handled by vertex shaders.

Silverlight is similar to WPF in many respects when it comes to shaders. Silverlight supports pixel shaders like WPF. It doesn't support vertex shaders directly. Instead, it uses XNA integration for 3D rendering. The Silverlight team chose to embrace the XNA framework and integrate it into their specifications, rather than write their own 3D engine. If you are an experienced XNA developer, you should have no problem adapting to the Silverlight version.

In Silverlight, pixel shaders are always executed on the CPU. In fact, the rasterizer also runs on the CPU.

WPF, on the other hand, runs the shaders on the GPU, falling back to CPU only in rare cases. Because Silverlight uses the CPU, you might worry about performance. You may suspect that Silverlight is slower when processing shaders and you'd be correct. Silverlight mitigates some of the performance woes by running shaders on multiple cores (when available) and by using the CPU's fast SSE instruction set. Yes, Silverlight shaders are slower than their WPF counterparts. When it comes to pixel manipulation, though, Silverlight shaders are still the fastest option, beating other venues like WriteableBitmap by a substantial margin. If you want to see the performance ramifications for yourself, René Schulte has an illuminating Silverlight performance demo that you should check out when you have the time: *http://kodierer.blogspot.com/2009/08/silverlight-3-writea blebitmap.html*

Summary

Pixel shaders have revolutionized the computer graphics industry. The powerful special effects and digital landscapes shown in modern movies and games would not be possible without them. Adobe Photoshop and other designer applications are jammed with effects that are implemented with pixel shaders. They are a magnificent way to create your own custom effects. Granted, the HLSL syntax is a bit cumbersome and difficult to understand at first, but it's worth learning. Once you master HLSL, you can create shaders for DirectX, XNA, WPF, Silverlight, and Windows 8 Metro. In the next chapter, I'll show you how to create your first XAML shader project. By the end of this book, you'll be able to add the title "HLSL ninja" to your resume.

CHAPTER 2

Getting Started

In this chapter, you get your first look at using shaders in an XAML application. Using the prebuilt shaders in .NET is a snap. It's not much harder than using a drag and drop UI designer. You will also get a miniature tutorial on creating a simple custom shader.

Setting Up Your Development Computer

If you are a .NET developer, you know a lot about managed code and the .NET framework libraries. If Microsoft statistics are accurate, you write your code in either C# or Visual Basic. Moreover, if you are like me, you are a Visual Studio junkie, spending countless hours living inside the Visual Studio environment. Given these facts and the possibility that you are also an experienced XAML developer, it's likely that you already have your computer ready to create HLSL shaders. But I'm going to be methodical and show you what you need to make sure your development computer is set up correctly.

Silverlight Development

One thing you can say about the Silverlight team: they produce high-quality releases on a tight schedule. Silverlight 5 is the newest version available at this time. It requires a Visual Studio 2010 installation in order to build a Silverlight 5 project. If you are cheap, all you need is a copy of the free Visual Web Developer 2010 Express edition (*http://www.microsoft.com/express/web/*) to be ready to create Silverlight applications. If you have access to your corporate credit card, buy Visual Studio 2010 pro, premium or ultimate. You get a lot more tools in these editions and they are indispensable for real world development. To be fair, though, there is nothing in the more expensive editions that makes HLSL development any easier.

Since Silverlight 5 shipped after Visual Studio 2010, you need to visit *http://www.silver light.net/getting-started* and install the Silverlight 5 tools and SDK before you are completely ready to start coding.

WPF Development

To get the most out of your shader code, use the .NET 4.0 version of WPF. That's because 4.0 supports a more recent shader specification (*PS_3_0*) and that gives you more shader power. For the skinflints in the audience, look at the Visual C# 2010 Express (*http://bit.ly/VCS2010Express*) or Visual Basic 2010 Express (*http://bit.ly/VB2010Express*) editions. Both express editions are fully capable of creating WPF applications and incorporating your shader code. Just like with Silverlight 5, you can use the commercial editions of Visual Studio for development (*http://bit.ly/wEUD17*).

The Visual Studio install takes about an hour. I suspect most readers have gone through the installation process many times so I'll assume you know what you are doing and don't need step by step instructions.

Expression Blend 4

I highly recommend that XAML developers learn Expression Blend (*http://bit.ly/expres sionblend4/*). It contains dozens of tools that simplify XAML UI development and it is a perfect companion for Visual Studio. For the shader developer, it is useful for two reasons. First, it ships with a nice set of prebuilt shader effects. Second, it provides a preview feature, making it easy to see the effect without having to run the application first.

Installing Blend is a ten-minute exercise. Download the installer from the Microsoft site and follow the prompts.

Choosing a Shader Compiler

Your HLSL shader source code is just text; any text editor will suffice for code creation. Before you can use the shader, it must be compiled into a binary file and added to the GPU during runtime. Thus, you need a compiler.

DirectX Compiler

Visual Studio is such a powerhouse that many assume it has compilers for any programming language, but neither Visual Studio 2010 nor Expression Blend 4 includes a shader compiler. There is good news on the horizon though; the next version of Visual Studio has some remarkable 3D editors, and it will have a shader compiler. In the meantime, you need to find a compiler before you can continue.

Since HLSL is a part of DirectX you can use the FXC.exe compiler in the DirectX SDK. FXC.exe is a small file; it's less than 200KB in size. Regrettably, the FXC compiler is only available as part of the SDK and that SDK is a monster, using up over one gigabyte of your hard drive space.

I use the FXC compiler for some of the examples in this book. If you want to follow along, you can find the DirectX SDK at *http://msdn.microsoft.com/directx/*.

WPF Build Task

The good folks on the WPF team have a few open source projects on Codeplex (*http://wpf.codeplex.com/*). If you snoop around their Codeplex site, you'll find a shader build task that doesn't require having the DirectX SDK installed (*http://wpf.codeplex.com/releases/view/14962/*). Here's what is does. If it is installed it enhances the normal MSBuild build process. It looks for any files with an *.fx* extension within your WPF project. It compiles the source in that *.fx* file into a binary file (**.ps*). It has two exasperating limitations, however: it is not available for Silverlight projects and it doesn't compile to the newer PS_3_0 specifications.

Shazzam Shader Editor

Shazzam Shader Editor is a free standalone tool for writing XAML shaders (Figure 2-1). If you install Shazzam, you don't need to install the massive DirectX SDK, as it has its own compiler. It contains an HLSL code editor that has intellisense and code completion. That might not seem like a big deal until you learn that Visual Studio doesn't have intellisense for HLSL files. Earlier in this chapter, I mentioned the effect preview feature in Expression Blend. Shazzam does Blend one better, featuring a spate of preview, animation, and comparison features. Shazzam has been available for the last four years and has thousands of users around the world. It's the recommended shader tool in nearly every Silverlight book on the market.

I have to tell you, in the interest of full disclosure, I'm the primary developer for Shazzam. Of course I think it's the best tool available for learning XAML specific HLSL. I encourage you to download a free copy from *http://shazzam-tool.com* and see for yourself. I use Shazzam extensively throughout this book, so be sure and read Chapter 6 to learn more about the tool.

To install Shazzam, download the installer from shazzam-tool.com (*http://shazzam-tool.com*) and follow the prompts. The install takes less than a minute on most computers.

Other Tools to Consider

FX Composer

NVidia has a stake in the shader community and has a number of developer tools. One of their more impressive applications is the FX Composer tool. It is aimed squarely at the game development community and has tons of remarkable features. It boasts a

Figure 2-1. Shazzam Shader Editor IDE

shader debugger, supports easy importation of 3D models, has a particle system generator, test harness, and many other cool enhancements (Figure 2-2).

It's an impressive tool, but I find it overkill for creating pixel shaders for Silverlight or WPF. You can find it on the NVidia site at *http://developer.nvidia.com/fx-composer/*.

NShader

NShader (*http://nshader.codeplex.com/*) is a Visual Studio extension, which provides syntax highlighting for assorted shader languages including HLSL, Cg and GLSL. If you write HLSL in Visual Studio, you may find this tool useful. It's strangely incomplete, though, and misses some obvious HLSL functions like `sampler2D()`.

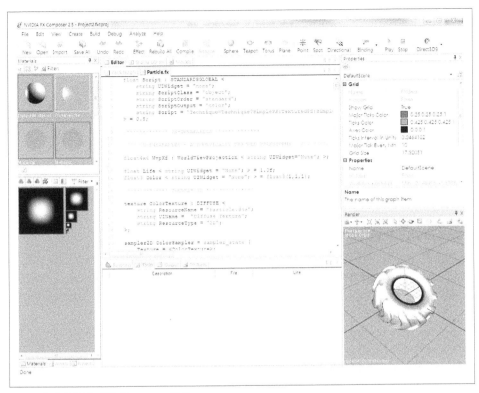

Figure 2-2. NVidia FX Composer IDE

Visual Studio 2012

I've looked at the 3D tools included in Visual Studio 2012 (which ships sometime in 2012) and I'm impressed. Download a free copy of the developer preview (*http://bit.ly/vs2012download*) to see what's coming.

A First Shader Project

Traditionally, the first application in most programming books is the ubiquitous "hello world" application. Boring! I'll have none of that dreary code in this book. The cynical reader will point out that writing text to the screen with a shader is nearly impossible, but let's not go there. I need a graphical demo that shows a shader in action, but is also graphical in nature. With that in mind, I decided to make the first project an image transition application.

I want to say a couple of words about terminology before going any further. The terms *shader* and *effect* are pervasive and often used interchangeably. On the .NET side of the aisle, the common term is *effect*. Examine the UIElement class and you'll see that it has an Effect dependency property. Tour the class libraries and you'll discover the prebuilt DropShadowEffect and BlurEffect classes tucked amidst the other familiar XAML types. In addition, there is the ShaderEffect base class, which is used when creating your own custom effects.

On the HLSL side of the house, the word effect has special meaning; in this realm, you can think of an effect as a *shader package* containing multiple shaders targeting different hardware. The shader is the actual algorithm run on the GPU. To summarize, when you write a custom effect, you create a .NET effect class and an HLSL shader.

Using Prebuilt Effects

Silverlight and WPF have two built-in effects: *dropshadow* and *blur*. These effects are applicable to any UIElement, which includes any element in the visual tree. When an effect is applied to an element, it affects the element and all of its children elements. In our first project, you'll place the effect on an Image element.

To begin, open your Visual Studio edition and choose File→New Project from the menu bar (or press Ctrl-Shift-N). The New Project dialog opens, offering a number of options, as shown in Figure 2-3.

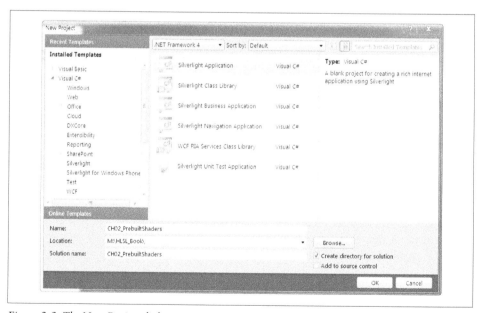

Figure 2-3. The New Project dialog

Select the Silverlight Application template. Enter a name of your choosing and click OK. Visual Studio will start creating a Silverlight application for you.

The New Silverlight Application dialog box will appear, asking whether you want to host the application in a new website (Figure 2-4). For simple Silverlight applications, I rarely create a host web project, so I recommend unselecting that check box. Leave the other options set to their defaults for now and click OK.

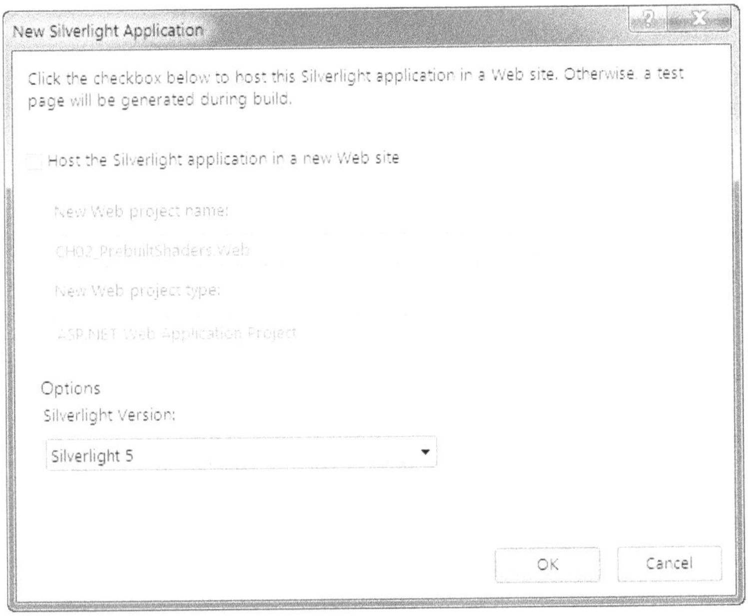

Figure 2-4. New Silverlight Application dialog

Use the Project→Add Existing Item menu bar to add a couple of image files to the project.

Next, open the *MainPage.xaml* file and modify the following values on the UserControl element.

```
d:DesignHeight="600" d:DesignWidth="800"
```

Setting the DesignHeight and DesignWidth properties makes it easier to see the images on the Visual Studio designer.

Add the following XAML to the *MainPage.xaml* files (Example 2-1).

Example 2-1. Add Images and Slider XAML

```
<Grid x:Name="LayoutRoot"
      Background="White">
  <Grid.RowDefinitions>
```

```
        <RowDefinition Height='380' />
        <RowDefinition Height='40' />
    </Grid.RowDefinitions>
    <!-- set the Source to a valid path in your project -->
    <Image x:Name='StartImage'
            Source='garden1.jpg'
            Width='500'
            Opacity='1'></Image>

    <!-- set the Source to a valid path in your project -->
    <Image x:Name='EndImage'
            Source='garden2.jpg'
            Width='480'
            Opacity='0'></Image>
    <Slider x:Name='TransitionSlider'
            Grid.Row='1'
            Width='500' />
</Grid>
```

The XAML in Example 2-1 creates two Image elements, one superimposed over the
other. The width of the EndImage is smaller than the StartImage to accentuate the transition. There is also a Slider element, located at the bottom of the grid, which is used
to control the transition amount.

Figure 2-5 shows what the UI looks like at this stage:

Figure 2-5. Transition project, phase 1

In the next phase, you will add a couple lines of code to fade between the two images
when the slider is moved. Start by adding a ValueChanged event handler to the existing
XAML. Experienced XAML developers know that Visual Studio shows a *New Event*

Handler prompt (Figure 2-6) when adding event attributes in the XAML editor. Pressing Tab at the prompt stubs in the correct attributes value and writes an event procedure in the code behind.

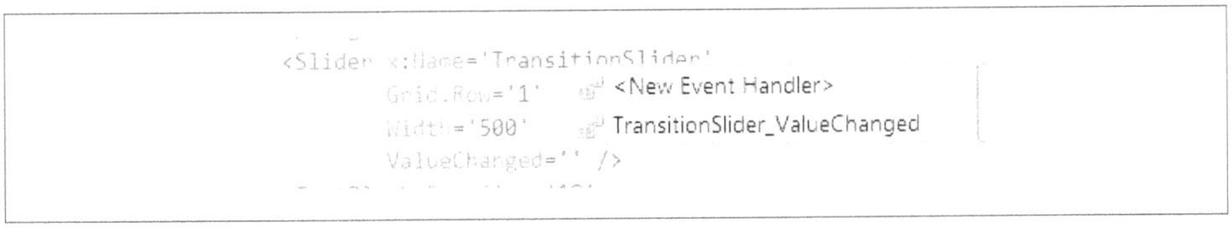

```
<Slider x:Name='TransitionSlider'
        Grid.Row='1'      <New Event Handler>
        Width='500'       TransitionSlider_ValueChanged
        ValueChanged='' />
```

Figure 2-6. The Insert New Event Handler prompt

When you are done, your XAML for the slider should look like Example 2-2.

Example 2-2. ValueChanged event text

```
<Slider x:Name='TransitionSlider'
        Grid.Row='1'
        Width='500'
        ValueChanged='TransitionSlider_ValueChanged' />
```

Press F7 to switch to the code behind view and add the following code to the C# file (Example 2-3).

Example 2-3. The TransitionSlider_ValueChanged event code

```
private void TransitionSlider_ValueChanged(object sender,
                RoutedPropertyChangedEventArgs<double> e) {
  // transition the images
  var max = TransitionSlider.Maximum;
  EndImage.Opacity = e.NewValue / max;
  StartImage.Opacity = 1 - EndImage.Opacity;
}
```

As you can see, this code changes the opacity of the two Image elements. Opacity accepts a value between 0.0 and 1.0, so the code uses a calculation to normalize the current slider value to that range.

```
    e.NewValue / max
```

The last line ensures that when `StartImage.Opacity` is at 0.0, the `EndImage.Opacity` is set to 1.0, and vice versa.

```
    StartImage.Opacity = 1 - EndImage.Opacity;
```

Run the application and drag the slider to change the value. The first image gradually disappears as the second image fades into view.

Adding Effects

To make the transition more interesting, you can apply a BlurEffect during the fade-in and fade-out. The BlurEffect is a nice choice for your first look at a built-in effect. It's one of the built-in effects, it's available for Silverlight and WPF, and it's quite simple to use. There are different types of blur effects used in the graphics industry (motion blur, zoom blur, Gaussian blur). The BlurEffect class is one of the simplest implementations, providing a uniform unfocused look to the affected pixels. If you've ever looked through a frosted translucent screen, you've seen the effect.

 The BlurEffect uses a simplistic blur algorithm, which is effective but slower than other potential blur implementations. A custom BoxBlur or optimized Gaussian Blur outperforms the built-in WPF blur.

Each UIElement has an Effect property. In this project, the potential candidates for the effect are the UserControl, Grid, Slider, and the two Image elements. When you apply an effect to a parent element, like the Grid, it affects all the children elements. Each element can have only one effect set directly in its Effect property but can inherit other effects from its parents. Imagine applying a BlurEffect to the parent Grid (Layout Root) and an InvertColorEffect to StartImage. StartImage would have both effects applied, while EndImage would show only the blur effect.

The BlurEffect has one interesting property: *Radius*. You can think of Radius as the strength of the blur effect. The higher the Radius value, the fuzzier the output.

Here's how to add a BlurEffect in XAML (Example 2-4).

Example 2-4. Add BlurEffect in XAML

```
<Image x:Name='StartImage'
       Source='garden1.jpg'
       Width='500'
       Opacity='1'>
    <Image.Effect>
      <BlurEffect
         Radius='20' />
    </Image.Effect>
  </Image>
```

Of course, you can also apply the effect in the code behind (Example 2-5).

Example 2-5. Add BlurEffect in code

```
var blur = new System.Windows.Media.Effects.BlurEffect();
blur.Radius = 20;
StartImage.Effect = blur;
```

Now that the effect is applied, run the application. The UI should look similar to Figure 2-7.

Figure 2-7. Image element with blur effect

Are you ready to add the blur effect to the transition? Begin by setting the Radius value to zero for the existing blur effect. Then add a blur to the EndImage (Example 2-6).

Example 2-6. Blur effect for both images

```
<Image x:Name='StartImage'
       Source='garden1.jpg'
       Width='500'
       Opacity='1'>
  <Image.Effect>
    <BlurEffect x:Name='StartImageBlur'
                Radius='0' />
  </Image.Effect>
</Image>
<Image x:Name='EndImage'
       Source='garden2.jpg'
       Width='480'
       Opacity='0'>
  <Image.Effect>
    <BlurEffect x:Name='EndImageBlur'
                Radius='0' />
  </Image.Effect>
</Image>
```

Next, write some code to apply the blur gradually as the opacity level changes. Modify the ValueChanged event handler as follows (Example 2-7):

Example 2-7. Value Changed event procedure code

```
// transition the images
var max = TransitionSlider.Maximum;
EndImage.Opacity = e.NewValue / max;
StartImage.Opacity = 1 - EndImage.Opacity;

// opacity is between 0.0 and 1.0
// we want a max blur radius of 20 so will multiply
// by 20
StartImageBlur.Radius = EndImage.Opacity * 20;
EndImageBlur.Radius = StartImage.Opacity * 20;
```

The project is finished. Run the application and watch the transition. As the first image fades away, it gets blurrier, while the second image fades in and snaps into focus. Nice effect! (Pun intended.) I'll show you how to create a custom effect soon, but first, a word about performance.

Debrief

I have a few quibbles with this code: for one, the performance might be improved by consolidating the effects. There are two blur effects applied to an overlapped area of the screen. If you are seeing perf issues during testing, this is an area worthy of further research. To consolidate, you could remove the image effects, wrap the two Images inside another container, and apply the blur to the parent container. You can't use the current grid (LayoutRoot) because the blur would alter all children, including the slider element. The solution is to add another grid and place the images in the new grid. You'll have to change the transition code too.

Custom Shader

Now that you have some rudimentary experience working with a prebuilt effect, it's time to consider writing a custom one. Custom shaders are necessary when an existing effect doesn't do what you need. Let's say you read an article describing a faster blur algorithm and you decide to alter the BlurEffect to use the newer algorithm. If you wait for Microsoft to release a new version, who knows how long you'll have to wait? In this situation, you are better off writing your own effect.

For your first custom shader, I picked a simple color modification effect. The shader code is childishly simple, just to give you an overview of the custom shader process. I promise there are more details coming as you read deeper into this book.

There are a few common steps necessary for creating a custom shader:

- Create a text file containing your HLSL code.
- Compile the HLSL into a binary file.
- Add the binary shader file to an XAML project and mark it as a project resource.
- Create a .NET wrapper class to expose the shader to your project.
- Compile the project.
- Instantiate your shader and assign it to an element Effect property.

Create a Shader Algorithm

Crafting a custom shader starts by creating a text file and adding some HLSL code. Example 2-8 shows how to write a simple InvertColor shader.

Example 2-8. HLSL code for InvertColor shader

```
sampler2D InputTexture;

float4 main(float2 uv : TEXCOORD) : COLOR {
    float4 color = tex2D( InputTexture, uv );
    float4 invertedColor = float4(color.a - color.rgb, color.a);

    return invertedColor;
}
```

There is not much code in this example, but it's sufficient to reverse the color on every pixel in the input stream.

The first line declares the input source, InputTexture, for the shader.

```
sampler2D InputTexture;
```

In your sample application, this InputTexture corresponds to pixels contained in the Image elements. Next is a function declaration.

```
float4 main(float2 uv : TEXCOORD) : COLOR {
```

As you can see, the function is named main and returns a float4 value. That float4 represents the color value for the modified pixel, which is destined for the computer screen. You can think of a float4 as containing four values corresponding to the color values (red, green, blue, alpha). The next two lines sample a pixel from the input source and calculate the new output color, which is stored in the invertedColor variable.

```
float4 color = tex2D( InputTexture, uv );
float4 invertedColor = float4(color.a - color.rgb, color.a);
```

Finally, the inverted color is returned from the function call.

```
return invertedColor;
```

Compile the HLSL Code

Next, it is necessary to compile the `InvertColor` shader code into a binary file. By convention, this binary file ends with a *.ps* extension. There are a number of ways to compile shader source code. For this first walkthrough, you will use the FXC.EXE compiler that ships with the DirectX SDK. If you have the SDK installed, you can open a DirectX command prompt from the Windows Start menu as shown in Figure 2-8.

Figure 2-8. The DirectX Command prompt on the Start menu

At the DirectX prompt, run the FXC compiler with this entry.

```
fxc /T ps_2_0 /E main /Fo output.ps invertcolor.txt
```

The compiler takes the code in the *invertcolor.txt* file and compiles it into the *output.ps* file. There are various switches specified that tell the compiler to use the `main` function as the shader entry point and to compile with the ps_2_0 shader specification.

Be forewarned: FXE is finicky about encoding types for the input file. It prefers ASCII and doesn't like Unicode encoded text files.

Add to Visual Studio XAML Project

The next step in the process is to add the ps file to an XAML project. Be sure and set the Build Action for the file to Resource as shown in Figure 2-9.

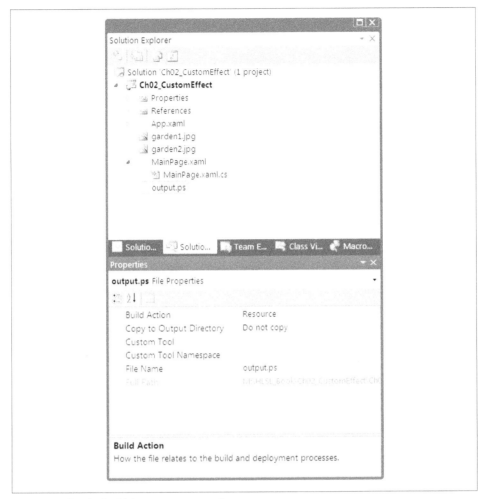

Figure 2-9. Set the Build Action property to Resource

Create a .NET Wrapper Class

To use a pixel shader, you need a way for .NET code to interact with it. The prescribed means to accomplish this is to write a wrapper class. The class derives from the ShaderEffect base class and exposes dependency properties to manipulate shader properties. The simple InvertColor shader doesn't provide any shader properties, so the example wrapper class will be small.

Add a class to the project and insert the following code (Example 2-9).

Example 2-9. InvertColorEffect wrapper class

```
public class InvertColorEffect : ShaderEffect
  {
    private PixelShader pixelShader = new PixelShader();

    public InvertColorEffect() {

      pixelShader.UriSource =
        new Uri("/Ch02_CustomEffect;component/output.ps", UriKind.Relative);
      this.PixelShader = pixelShader;

      this.UpdateShaderValue(InputProperty);
    }

    public static readonly DependencyProperty InputProperty =
      ShaderEffect.RegisterPixelShaderSamplerProperty("Input",
        typeof(InvertColorEffect), 0);

    // represents the InputSource for the shader
    public Brush Input {
      get {
        return ((Brush)(this.GetValue(InputProperty)));
      }
      set {
        this.SetValue(InputProperty, value);
      }
    }
  }
}
```

You may recall that the .NET wrapper must instruct Silverlight or WPF to load the binary resource. In WPF, the binary is loaded into the GPU; in Silverlight, it's loaded into the virtualized GPU. You can see the loader code in the constructor.

```
pixelShader.UriSource =
        new Uri("/Ch02_CustomEffect;component/output.ps",
            UriKind.Relative);
```

There is also a single dependency property name `InputProperty`. This property represents the input into the shader. In other words, it's the data provided by the rasterizer. The dependency property follows the XAML convention and looks like you would expect, with one small difference.

```
public static readonly DependencyProperty InputProperty =
        ShaderEffect.RegisterPixelShaderSamplerProperty("Input",
            typeof(InvertColorEffect), 0);
```

The `ShaderEffect.RegisterPixelShaderSampler` property is how the dependency property is associated with the pixel shader sampler register. Don't fret too much about the details of this class for now. It's ready to compile.

Compile the Project

Build the project and verify that everything compiles.

Instantiate the Shader

How do you want add the InvertColorEffect to the image? If you want to add it in code, you just instantiate the effect and assign it to the correct element property.

```
var invert = new InvertColorEffect();
StartImage.Effect = invert;
```

To add the effect in your XAML file, add a custom XML namespace to the UserControl. This xmlns should reference the .NET namespace that contains your wrapper class.

```
<UserControl x:Class="Ch02_CustomEffect.MainPage"
             xmlns="http://schemas.microsoft.com/winfx/2006/xaml/presentation"
             xmlns:x="http://schemas.microsoft.com/winfx/2006/xaml"
             xmlns:d="http://schemas.microsoft.com/expression/blend/2008"
             xmlns:mc="http://schemas.openxmlformats.org/markup-compatibility/2006"
             xmlns:local='clr-namespace:Ch02_CustomEffect'
             mc:Ignorable="d" >
```

Then apply the effect to the image.

```
<Image x:Name='StartImage'
       Source='garden1.jpg'
       Width='500'
       Opacity='1'>
    <Image.Effect>
      <local:InvertColorEffect />
    </Image.Effect>
</Image>
```

Be sure and comment out the code in the TransitionSlider_ValueChanged event handler or you will get a runtime error.

Figure 2-10 is what the InvertColorEffect looks like when you run the application.

Figure 2-10. InvertColorEffect applied to image

Summary

Effects are one of the strong points of XAML development. As a former Windows Forms developer, I struggled with the severe limitations of GDI programming and I never want to go back. I embrace the new rendering capabilities in WPF and Silverlight with gusto and appreciate the benefits provide by the custom shader API.

Welcome to the marvelous world of shader development.

Shader Scenario

You are working on a Silverlight project for a large media client. Its lead designer is fascinated with steampunk and insists that the spring campaign reflect his new love. In conjunction with the promotion is a user submitted product video contest. Winners of the best video will take home a cash prize. Your job is to create the video viewer for the contest entries. But there is a requirement that is making your manager anxious: all the videos need to look like movies from the early 1900s. None of the submitted videos have the correct look and there is no budget for video post-production on the submissions.

Shader Solution

The solution, of course, is to create an old movie shader. The shader takes the video output, converts it to a monotone color, and tints it an antique brown tone. Next, it applies a vignette mask to the output. Vignette is a photography term that describes an effect often seen in wedding shots and other glamour pictures. The corners of the picture are tinted slightly darker than the center of the image.

Just apply the old movie shader to the video player output and you are done.

CHAPTER 3

Commonplace Pixel Shaders

"What is an example of a real world pixel shader?" That's a question I hear all the time when teaching the concepts of shaders to XAML programmers. The trouble, as I see it, is that most computer users wouldn't recognize a pixel shader if they saw one. Make no mistake, they are out there—pixel shaders are found in a wide range of software products. Most consumers happily use them without knowing that they are working with a feature that was implemented with an effect.

Certain application categories are prime candidates for pixel shaders. The game development world is one obvious example. Image manipulation software is another fertile area for shaders. Academics have studied the problem of image filtering and pixel manipulation for decades. All modern image processing software (think Photoshop or Paintshop Pro) has ranks of shaders hiding behind the application facade.

Common effects include blurring, distorting, image enhancement, and color blend. This chapter provides an overview of the types of effects that are common in the shader realm.

 Shaders are often applied after the render phase, so they are also known as post-processing effects.

Pixel shaders fall into a few general categories.

- Color modification / Color transformation
- Displacement / Spatial transformation
- Blurs
- Generative / Procedural
- Multiple inputs

A Word About Pseudocode

A couple of words before diving into the shader descriptions. It is still early in the book and you haven't seen a lot of HLSL syntax. With that in mind, most of the code listed in this chapter is pseudocode, which is useful for explaining the general idea behind a shader implementation but doesn't use the official HLSL syntax. Here is a simple example.

Example 3-1. Pseudocode and HLSL compared

```
// pseudocode
originalColor = color.r
average   = (color.r + color.b + color.g)/3

// HLSL syntax
float4 originalColor = tex2D(InputTexture, uv);
originalColor = color.r ;

float average;
average = color.rgb/3;
```

The HLSL in this example is more precise than the pseudocode version of that same code. First, it gets the color using the **text2D** function. Then, it defines the variables with the **float4** and **float** keywords. Leaving the last line to employ the HLSL *swizzle* syntax to calculate the average.

 Swizzling, in HLSL, provides a unique way to access members of a vector. While the word conjures images of fruity drinks around a tropical pool, it's just a way to perform operations on any combination of vector items.

Our Sample Image

For many of the examples in this chapter, I will use the color photo you see in Figure 3-1. I picked this photo because it is colorful and has a nice composition. Furthermore, it has a black background, which works well with some of the color replacement shaders.

Color Modification

Color modification is a simple concept. Take an incoming pixel color and shift that color according to a given formula. What's key to understanding this category of pixel shaders is that the basic image structure stays the same. The algorithm doesn't move or reposition pixels on the screen. Take a picture of a cat, for example; you'll know that it's a cat, even though the colors are translated into shades of purple and blue.

Figure 3-1. Flower photo with no effect applied

Common Techniques

Color correction is one use of color modification that is indispensable to the film and print industry. Most of the images you see on television or in a magazine have been color-corrected during post-production. Whether it was to adjust contrast on a marginal exposure, create unified skin tones for a fashion spread, or apply a gloomy color palette to a Gothic novel poster, most commercial imagery undergoes color alteration before it is released for public consumption. Color corrections largely come in two flavors: per-channel corrections, which alter red, green, and blue components independently; and color-blending procedures, in which the output value is determined based on combined values in the RGB channels.

Stylizing a photo is another popular color modification technique, such as utilizing sepia tone and tinting, introducing sixties-era colors, making an image look like it's from an old movie, inverting colors, or using color channels.

Color removal is another commonplace technique. Grayscale and desaturation are popular methods that fall into this category.

Photo editing applications are rife with tools in this category. Open your copy of Adobe Photoshop and look in the Image→Adjustments menu (Figure 3-2). It's packed with color adjustment tools and it's likely that a pixel shader or two is employed behind the scenes to do the real work.

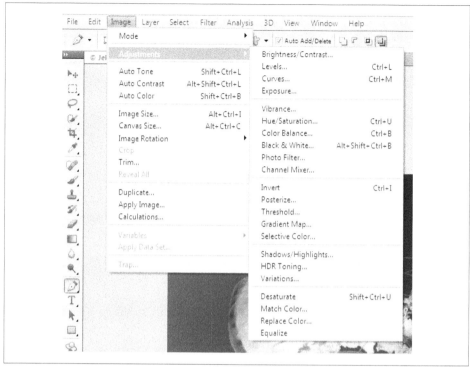

Figure 3-2. Photoshop Adjustments Menu

Black, White, and Gray

All the shaders in this subsection remove the natural colors from the image and replace them with a monotone value. Creating a grayscale image is accomplished by setting a color value that consists of equal parts of the red, green, and blue channels.

It's likely that you know this already; nevertheless, a quick review is in order. A pixel with each RGB color set to zero results in a black pixel.

```
newColor = color.rgb(0,0,0); // pseudocode
```

When each RGB value is set to one, the output renders as a white pixel.

```
newColor = color.rgb(1,1,1); // pseudocode
```

Whenever all three RGB values are set to the same value, a gray pixel is produced.

```
newColor = color.rgb(0.2, 0.2, 0.2); // pseudocode
```

HLSL shaders normalize color values to the range 0–1, as you can see in the following example (Example 3-2).

Example 3-2. Setting grayscale values

```
// pseudocode
RGB(0, 0, 0); // black
RGB(1, 1, 1); // white
RGB(0.8, 0.8, 0.8); // light gray
RGB(0.2, 0.2, 0.2); // dark gray
```

Black-White

You've seen black and white photos in fine art magazines or your local gallery. In most cases, they are not pure black and white, though; they are composed of multiples shades of gray. True black and white is rare but is occasionally used for dramatic effect.

Technique: This shader works by setting all pixels over a certain threshold to white and the rest of the pixels to black (Example 3-3).

Example 3-3. Black-white pseudocode

```
if (color.r > .5) // use the red channel for threshold trigger
{ RGB(1,1,1);}
else
{ RGB(0,0,0);}
```

Check out Figure 3-3, a reductionist version of our original image created with a shader using the black-white technique.

Grayscale

Grayscale images appear to have no color, only tones of gray. Other common names for this image type are monochromatic and monotone.

Technique: The shader must examine the pixel and decide what value to assign to the RGB channels. One approach is to use a single channel at the filter (See Figure 3-4.a and 3.4.b). For example, take the red value and assign it to the green and blue channels.

Another approach is to average the color channels and apply the average to each RGB value (see Figure 3-4.c). For the most realistic approach, however, don't use a simple average calculation. The lab-coated masterminds at ICC provide a nice weighting formula that makes your grayscale feel authentic (see Figure 3-4.d).

```
// pseudocode
gray = RGB(inputColor * 0.21, inputColor * 0.71, inputColor * 0.07)
```

 The human eye is more sensitive to the green spectrum than other colors. Using a grayscale formula that enhances the green spectrum results in an image that looks closer to a picture taken with black and white film.

Figure 3-3. Black and white effect

Color Replacement

Effects in this category seek out a color and substitute another in its place. These effects usually have a color sensitivity dial, which tweaks how precisely you wish to match the target color.

Other names for these effects are *ColorKey* and *ChromaKey*. In the samples included with this book is one called *ColorKeyAlpha*. It transforms any pixel of the target color to a transparent value (by setting the Alpha channel to zero).

All sci-fi and action movie buffs are familiar with green screen effects, whereby the actors work in front of a dazzling lime-green screen and the bellowing velociraptor is added to the scene in post-production. A ChromaKey effect is a form of color replacement. Because the replacement data is not a simple color but a complex image, ChromaKey can also be categorized as a multi-input effect. That's because the effect relies on having at least two samples passed into the shader: the foreground image where the actors live, and the background image where the dinosaurs roam.

Color Enhancement and Correction

How many times have you taken a picture indoors and been dismayed to see a blue cast on the finished picture? Fluorescent lights are to blame, as they use an unnatural

(a) Grayscale based on green channel

(b) Grayscale based on red channel

(c) Grayscale based on simple average

(d) Grayscale based on ICC weighting

Figure 3-4. Grayscale effect, based on different algorithms

light spectrum. Professional photographers understand the nuances of light and learn how to exploit it for their craft. But even they occasionally make mistakes during photo shoots and need to correct the image in post-production.

Color enhancement and correction can be achieved by applying one or several of the following techniques:

- Gloom
- Hue
- Saturation
- Contrast
- Brightness
- Bright Extract
- Bloom
- Color Balance
- Vibrance

- Thresholding
- LightStreak
- Tone Mapping

If you are familiar with image processing techniques, you will recognize some of the names in this list and perhaps know what they do when applied to a picture. Other terms, like Gloom, may be unfamiliar. In case you are curious, the Gloom effect intensifies the dark areas of the image.

This chapter mentions a lot of shader effects by name but there isn't enough room to provide a comprehensive catalog of every effect cited. They are all included in Shazzam; I encourage you to try them for yourself.

Distinctive Effects

Sometimes you just want to do something wacky to the output, like make the image look frosty or apply a cartoon color palette. Shaders can handle the job with ease.

Some examples are:

- Frosty Outline
- Old Movie
- Vignette
- ParametricEdgeDetection
- Tinting
- Color Tone
- Pixelation
- Sketch
- Pencil
- Toon

The Pixelate effect (Figure 3-5.a) is used to simulate a close-up of an image, causing it to appear coarser, blockier and less detailed. The Old Movie effect (Figure 3-5.a) is a combination effect. It applies a sepia tone to the image. It also uses a vignette effect, whereby the pixels closer to the image perimeter are darkened. The Parametric Edge Detection effect (Figure 3-5.c) uses a convolution algorithm to detect edges of items within the image. In this version, it colors the edges with vibrant colors to make them stand out. The last effect (Figure 3-5.d) transforms the image into a version that looks like it was hand sketched with a pencil.

(a) Pixelate Effect

(b) Old Movie Effect

(c) Parametric Edge Detection Effect

(d) Sketch Effect

Figure 3-5. Shader Effects

Distortion and Displacement

Shaders in this category are less subtle than the color modification examples. They aggressively move pixels around the screen, causing bulges and ripples to appear on an otherwise flat output. Generally, the objective is to trick the user's brain into seeing a real-world distortion where none exists.

The techniques used are diverse but all have one thing in common. When determining the color to use for an output pixel, they don't use the color from its current position. They borrow the color from a neighboring pixel or interpolate a new output color based upon calculations run on nearby locations.

Be attentive when looking at HLSL code on the Internet, as a good portion of your search results are likely vertex shader examples. This is particularly true when researching displacement shaders and lighting shaders. As you may recall, vertex shaders are a companion type of shader that are part of the DirectX input pipeline. Whereas pixel shaders change pixel colors, a vertex shader interacts with the 3D model vertex points. Typically, a vertex shader precedes a pixel shader in the shader pipeline. Many Internet examples consist of a mixture of the two with the majority of the work implemented in the vertex portion, which does us no good as we can only work with the pixel shader portion of the pipeline.

The terms applied to this technique are varied: distortion shaders, displacement mapping, per-pixel displacement, relief mapping, spatial transformation, and parallax mapping are some of the more common names. Let's look at some of these effects.

Magnify

The Magnify effect enlarges a subset of the image, zooming the user in for a closer look. The enlarged area is often elliptical, though I've seen other implementations.

Figure 3-6 shows the flower image, with two different magnification effects applied. The effect on the left has a hard edge to the enlargement area, while the one on the right uses a smoothing algorithm. The smoothing makes it appear more natural and glass-like. You may also see this called a bulge effect.

Figure 3-6. Two implementations of a magnify effect

Embossed

The embossed shader is a simple displacement shader. The photo processing community calls this the Inset effect. It provides a monocolor 3D appearance to the image. This is accomplished by making two separate monochrome versions of the image and making the first copy lighter in color than the second copy. Then the images are displaced a few pixels away from each other (See Figure 3-7.a). For example, the light version is moved two pixels to the left, the dark version two pixels to the right.

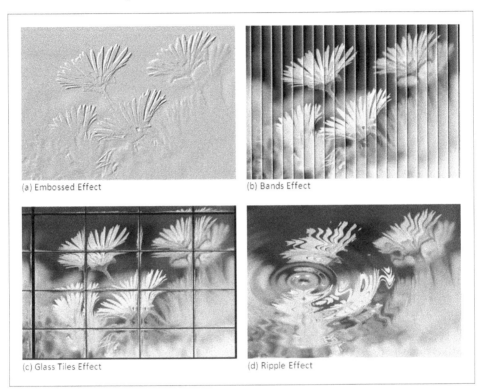

(a) Embossed Effect

(b) Bands Effect

(c) Glass Tiles Effect

(d) Ripple Effect

Figure 3-7. More distortion effects

Figure 3-7 presents a few more distortion effects. The Bands effect (Figure 3-7.b) appears to draw vertical blinds over the image. For a glassy, tiled look, choose the Glass Tiles effect (Figure 3-7.c) and the Ripple effect (Figure 3-7.d) provides the ubiquitous and overused water droplet effect.

Figure 3-8. Mirror effect

Testing Distortion Effects

I love the colors and composition of the flower image but it is a poor choice for testing certain distortion effects. However, it works well for testing the following mirror effect (Figure 3-8).

For effects like bulge or pinch, it's better to test with a hard-edged geometric pattern —I find that a checkerboard pattern works best. Figure 3-9 shows some sample effects applied to a black and white checkerboard.

Figure 3-9. Checkerboard with various distortion effects

Other Displacement Effects

Displacement shaders are a fertile area of development. Here is a listing of some of the more interesting effects in this category. You can see a few examples in Figure 3-9.

Just a few displacement shaders are:

- Paperfold
- Pivot
- Pixelate
- Splinter
- Camera Lens Correction
- Bulge
- Pinch
- Ripples
- Swirl
- Banded Swirl
- Bands
- Tiles
- Glass Tiles
- Mirror

Once again, I must omit the detailed descriptions of each of these effects. There isn't enough room in this book to cover them all.

Blurs

Blurs are a type of displacement effect. Rather than being dramatic, like a ripple effect, they tend to be subtler and affect a smaller area. Some of the common blurs are named after the technique used to create the blur. The Gaussian blur and GrowablePoisson-Disk effect fall into this bucket.

 The Gaussian and Poisson algorithms are named after their inventors' surnames, Johann Carl Friedrich Gauss and Siméon Denis Poisson.

Both Silverlight and WPF have a built-in blur effect. While it is serviceable, you might consider some of the alternative blur algorithms listed below for parts of your interface.

Motion Blur

Motion blur is the apparent streaking of quickly moving objects in a photo or video frame. It is an artifact of camera hardware limitations and appears when to trying to capture a moving object while using a too-slow shutter speed. The graphics industry makes frequent use of this handy effect during post-production work. You'll find it used in computer graphics, video games, traditional and 3D animation, and movie special effects. This effect is also called a directional blur.

Zoom Blur

This blur mimics the action of taking a picture while zooming the camera lens closer to the subject. This effect is also known as the telescopic blur.

Sharpening

This effect attempts to remove blurriness from the source image by increasing the edge contrast ratio (a well-known process for changing perceived image sharpness). This effect is also called the Unsharp Mask effect.

Generative Effects

Most of the time, your effect is dependent on the inbound raster image. There are times when it is advantageous for an effect to ignore the inbound pixels and generate its own independent output, as in Figure 3-10. Choose this route when the effect generated can benefit from the multi-core and parallelization power of the Graphics Processing Unit (GPU). There are examples found across the Internet showing blazing fast fractal generators. Fractal algorithms are a dead-end for the XAML developer, however. We are stuck with the PS_2 and PS_3 specification, which has an inadequate number of instructions available for recursive functions. These limits mean that you can create a Mandelbrot quickly, but it will be a superficial portrayal of the beauty of fractals.

 Each new version of the Pixel Shader specification provides significant upgrades over the previous version. To write HLSL code to exploit the newest PS specification (PS_5_0) you must use the DirectX API itself as there is no support for it in Silverlight/WPF. Silverlight supports the PS_2_0 spec and WPF supports the PS_2_0 and PS_3_0 versions. To learn more about the difference in these specifications, try this website: *http://en.wikipedia.org/wiki/HLSL*.

Even though robust fractal patterns are out of the question, you can generate gradients and fancy patterns.

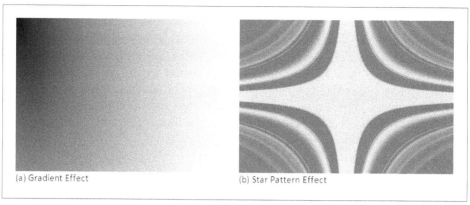

(a) Gradient Effect   (b) Star Pattern Effect

Figure 3-10. Generative effects

Multiple Inputs

Most of the effects seen in this chapter have been single input. To be more accurate, they have a single sampler input. Samplers, as you may recall, are the inbound pixels passed to the shader from the DirectX pipeline. You don't have to be clubbed with the obvious stick to recognize that if a shader has no input samples, it doesn't have much to work with.

 The generative shaders are the only useful effect that ignore input samplers.

The *PS_2* and *PS_3* specifications allow additional input samplers—up to a maximum of four in PS_2 and a maximum of eight in PS_3. You'll learn more about input samplers later in the book.

What can you do with multiple inputs? Here's a short list, though there are many more ideas to explore on your own.

- Sampler transition
- Color combination
- Texture map
- Photoshop blend modes

Sampler Transition

The last decade has seen pervasive changes in UI metaphors. Touch input is without a doubt the most transformative shift I've seen since starting my tech career. Another trendy change is transitional animation, whereby the user is moved from one state to another through a helpful animation. In the XAML world, this is frequently done with a storyboard. Let's envision a fade animation that transitions from a list of products to a products detail page. The accepted way to accomplish this in XAML is to layer the list UI over the detail UI and animate the opacity value of the top layer.

That's one way to accomplish a UI transition. Let's consider how you could implement this transition as a multi-input shader. You'd provide two inputs to the shader, one for each UI section. In the HLSL, you take the two inbound samplers and output one result. That result is either the first sampler, the second sampler, or some transitional value between the two. In your `.NET effect` class, provide a `Progress` dependency property. Then animate the `Progress` property and let the shader provide the fancy transition effect. Figure 3-11 shows a few stages of a transition effect implemented in this manner.

(a) Transition, 0% progress   (b) Transition, 20% progress

(c) Transition, 40% progress   (d) Transition, 60% progress

(e) Transition, 80% progress   (f) Transition, 100% progress

Figure 3-11. Multi-input shader, showing four stages of transition

Texture Map

Texture mapping takes the values stored in one input texture and uses them to manipulate other input textures. Let's look at an example that uses the values in a geometric pattern image to manufacture a glasslike embossing effect on the flowers image.

In the Figure 3-12 example, the Texture map is the five squares shown in Figure 3-12.a. The effect combines the purple pixels of the texture map with the flower pixels from the other image to create a glasslike texture overlay (Figure 3-12.b).

(a) Five Square shape   (b) ApplyTextureMap effect

Figure 3-12. Shape and final output for ApplyTextureMap effect

Mapping can also get more sophisticated; you can use the colors in the map file to recolor the target image. For this example, I've created a map file containing bands of colors (Figure 3-13).

Figure 3-13. The Source map file

Start on the left edge of Figure 3-13 and look at the first pixel on the top row. What color do you see? I see a lustrous emerald green. Continue moving right on the top row of pixels and you see green pixels for a short stretch, then a few yellow pixels, then green again, followed by a strip of black. The colors change as they move rightward but stay limited to the three colors (green, yellow, and black).

There are exactly 256 pixels in that first row and they are going to serve as a lookup table for a shader.

 Oftentimes, a map file is only one pixel high by 256 pixels wide. It might help to think of it as a one-dimensional array with 256 elements. The image in Figure 3-13 is actually 20 pixels high. That extra height serves no purpose for the shader, but it does make it easier to see the picture in a book!

Some of you are thinking ahead and know why there are 256 pixels in the first row. Yes, that's the number of unique gray values in an 8-bit grayscale color range. Now if you replace each pixel in a grayscale image with a lookup color from the color map, you are performing a texture mapping. Black is replaced with pixel[0], which on our texture map is green. White is replaced with pixel[255], which is also green. The other 254 gray values use the lookup color found at their respective locations. Figure 3-14 shows before and after versions of three images with the color map applied.

Wait a minute. The flower on the last row in Figure 3-14 isn't a grayscale image. How does that mapping work? It's quite simple if you recall the earlier discussion on creating monochromatic shaders. The shader code converts the pixels to grayscale values before applying the texture map.

 Examples and source code for of each of the shader types discussed in this chapter can be found in the Shazzam Shader Editor.

Color Combination

Color combining is straightforward. Take a pixel from the same location in multiple sources and combine into a new color. The color algorithm here is the key. For an overtly simple algorithm, just average the RGBA channels across all input sources (Example 3-4).

Example 3-4. Sample color combination shader

```
// pseudocode

color1 = GetColor(sourceA);
color2 = GetColor(sourceB);

combinedColor.r = (color1.r + color2.r) /2;
combinedColor.g = (color1.g + color2.g) /2;
combinedColor.b = (color1.b + color2.b) /2;
combinedColor.a = (color1.a + color2.a) /2;
```

(a) Radial Gradient, Grayscale

(b) With TextureMap Effect

(c) Test Image, Grayscale

(d) With TextureMap Effect

(e) Color Image

(f) With TextureMap Effect

Figure 3-14. Three images with texture map applied

This works but produces a low contrast and muddy output. A more desirable approach is to determine what kind of color combination is best for the intended image effect. Luckily, there is a set of well-tested and respected formulas available. I'm referring to the Adobe Photoshop blend-mode algorithms. You see, the Photoshop developers have been thinking about the problem for a long time. As a result, their color blend-mode implementation is top-notch.

 In many situations, your input samplers will not have the same dimensions. In that case, there won't be a one-to-one relationship between pixels. WPF and Silverlight handle this situation by enlarging the smaller source to match the larger.

Photoshop Blend Modes

Adobe Photoshop is considered by most design shops to be 'the' premier photo-editing tool and knowing how to exploit its toolset is a considered a badge of honor in the designer community. If you ask me to name the single most important feature in Photoshop, I would vote for the layers feature. Without layers, you'd be hard-pressed to make parts of your image editable and get any work done.

When you have multiple layers in a Photoshop project, you can configure how the pixels in an upper layer combine with the pixels on the next layer down the stack. This feature is called *Blending Mode*. On a many-layered project, conceptualizing each layer and its blend can get complex, so for this discussion, I'll assume that there are only two layers.

Before explaining the modes, it's helpful to define the three colors as defined in Photoshop documentation. The lower layer contains the *base color*, the upper layer contains the *blend color*, and the output color is termed the *result color*.

The current version of Photoshop boasts over twenty blend modes (see Figure 3-15) and each one uses a different formula to blend colors between layers. You can read details about each mode on the Adobe website (*http://adobe.ly/cs5blendmodes*).

Darken Modes

Each of these modes results a darkening of the base image.

- Darken
- Multiply
- Color Burn
- Linear Burn

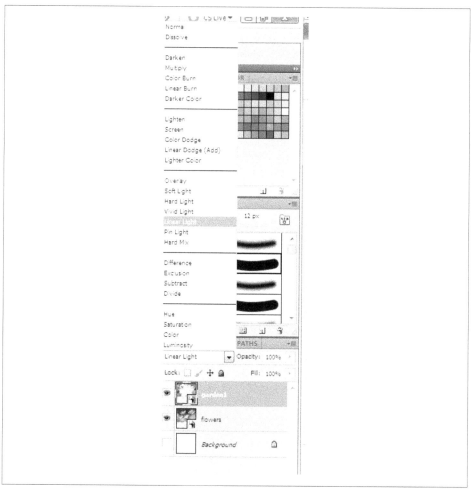

Figure 3-15. Photoshop blend modes

I'll examine the Darken blend mode here. A detailed discussion of all thirty modes is beyond the scope of this book, so I encourage you to learn more about the modes at the Adobe site.

The darken mode examines the base and blend colors for each pixel. The darker of the two is selected as the result color of that pixel. Figure 3-16 shows the results from using the four darken effects.

(a) Gray Canvas, base colors

(b) Head shot, blend colors

(c) Color Burn Effect

(d) Darken Effect

(e) LinearBurn Effect

(f) Multiply Effect

Figure 3-16. Darken blend modes

Lighten Modes

Each of these modes results in a lightening of the base image.

- Lighten
- Color Dodge
- Screen
- Linear Dodge

Contrast Modes

Each of the contrast modes lightens some pixels and darkens others in the base image, heightening the contrast.

- Hard Light
- Hard Mix
- Linear Light
- Overlay
- Pin Light
- Soft Light
- Vivid Light

Comparative Modes

Each of these modes compares the two layers, looking for regions that are identical in both.

- Difference
- Exclusion

Other Modes

Each of these modes uses a unique formula to blend the pixels. Some of these are addenda to the Photoshop blend algorithms and were provided by third-party tools or community members.

- Glow
- Negation
- Phoenix
- Reflect

Figure 3-17 shows a potpourri of blend effects.

(a) Hard Light Effect   (b) Hard Mix Effect

(c) Difference Effect   (d) Negation Effect

Figure 3-17. Sample of other blend effects

Blend Modes in HLSL

Recreating these blend modes in HLSL is a productive exercise and provides a great example of the usefulness of multiple input shaders. My favorite implementation of blend modes comes from Cory Plotts. His original library is available at *http://www .cplotts.com/2009/06/16/blend-modes-part-i/* and they are included in the latest Shazzam release.

Practical Uses for Shader Effects

It's a good bet that you are considering using custom effects in your application; otherwise, you'd not be reading this book. Effects are exciting and an obvious choice for certain families of applications (I'm thinking of the photo editors and video tools among other "fancy" UX applications).

Still, I suspect some readers are wondering about practical examples in business applications, so here are a few ideas to consider before you move into the next chapter.

Motion Blur in Moving Parts

Think about the parts of your UI that move. An obvious place to look is where you have animated elements. Adding a motion blur to the element while it is moving across the screen can make it seem livelier. It's done all the time in the movie and cartoon industry and it's worth considering in your application, too. Don't forget to consider other non-animated areas like listboxes and scrolling areas as candidates for motion blurs.

Blurs to Emphasize UI Focus

You can use a blur to focus attention toward a section of the UI. For example, when you show a Popup or Dialog in your application, apply a blur to the UI in the background. This will draw more attention to the dialog as the rest of the UI is blurry and the background appears to fade into the distance. Note that this technique works best when the main UI is maximized. I've used this technique for the dialogs in Shazzam Shader Editor. Check out Figure 3-18 to see a telescopic blur in action.

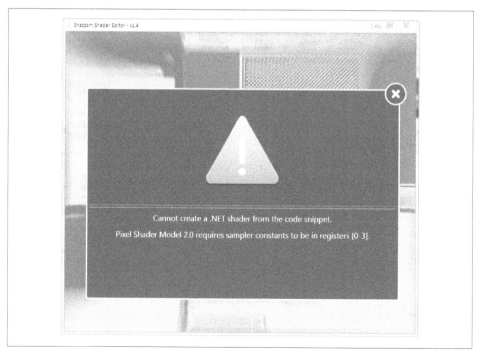

Figure 3-18. Using blur for dialog background

Desaturate for Emphasis

The Windows OS used this technique a few years back. When you switched from one OS theme another, the UI would desaturate slowly to gray, then saturate the colors back to your new theme. You could do a similar stunt in your application.

For example, reimagine the dialog shown in Figure 3-18 with a desaturated background, instead of the blurred one.

Summary

Creating a UI that is informative, yet delightful, is a delicate balancing act. On the practical side, you need input controls and access to the business data or the UI is just a pretty plaything. On the designer side, you want to follow time-tested design principles, choose beautiful typefaces and create an inspiring layout for the interface. Shaders are an enhancement to the designer mindset and provide unique tools for enriching an application. Be cautious when using bold effects or you might find your users are nauseated instead of elated with your rippling, oversaturated workspace. On the Silverlight side, you also need to consider the performance ramifications for shaders. Because they run on the CPU, Silverlight shaders are not as fast as their WPF brethren.

Shaders speak to my artistic side; I love the power and beauty inherent in these potent graphical nuggets. When I look at a shader example, my mind's eye sees the UI potential hiding in each effect. I'm sure you felt the tingle of inspiration while thumbing through the assortment of shader effects in this chapter. Now that you know what shaders can do, let's see how to use them in your Silverlight or WPF application.

CHAPTER 4

How WPF and Silverlight Use Shaders

You can spend your programming days happily working within the comforting confines of .NET's managed code libraries without ever seeing a smidgen of unmanaged code. The framework team is not stupid, though; they know there are times when you have to call out to a COM library or Win32 DLL to get your job done. So they created hooks in the framework to enable the flow of code between the sheltered world of managed code and the mysterious unmanaged realm. It's the same story when interoping between HLSL code and Silverlight/WPF classes.

In this chapter, we look at the .NET parts that facilitate the use of unmanaged HLSL shaders in the visual tree. The `UIElement.Effect` property is our first stop. It provides a way to assign a `ShaderEffect` to a visual element. Next, we look at some of the classes in the `System.Windows.Media.Effects` namespace. These classes (`ShaderEffect`, `Pixel Shader`, etc.) enable the flow of information to the HLSL world. We'll examine how to create your own managed wrappers for HLSL and investigate the prebuilt effects in the `System.Windows.Media.Effects` namespace and the Expression Blend libraries.

 Remember: on the .NET side, the customary term is *effect*; on the HLSL side, the preferred term is *shader*.

Framework Effects

It's easiest to start our discussion of framework effects by looking at the two shaders included in the `System.Windows.Media.Effects` namespace (see Figure 4-1). By starting with the `BlurEffect` and `DropShadowEffect`, we can concentrate on the XAML syntax and not worry about custom classes and resource management.

All visual elements derive from the `UIElement` class, which makes it an ideal location to surface the `Effect` property. With a few lines of XAML, you can apply an effect to any `UIElement`, as shown in Example 4-1.

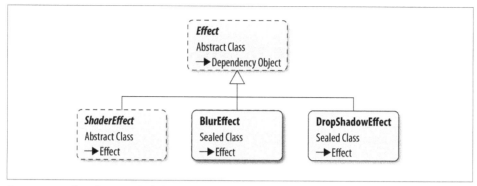

Figure 4-1. Effect classes included in the framework

Example 4-1. Applying BlurEffect to Image element

```
...
<Image Opacity='1'>
  <Image.Effect>
    <BlurEffect Radius='12' />
  </Image.Effect>
</Image>
...
```

BlurEffect

In an earlier chapter, I showed how to use the BlurEffect. It is one of the simpler effects. It applies a blur algorithm to the output, resulting in—you guessed it—a blurry output. The Silverlight version has one property, Radius, which influences the blurriness of the effect.

The WPF version adds two additional properties. The KernelType property is used to specify the blurring algorithm. The default algorithm is the infamous Gaussian blur. To switch to the simpler and less smooth Box kernel type, simply change the value as shown here (Example 4-2).

Example 4-2. Setting BlurEffect Properties

```
<CheckBox>
  <CheckBox.Effect>
    <BlurEffect KernelType='Box'
                RenderingBias='Quality' />
  </CheckBox.Effect>
</CheckBox>
```

There are tradeoffs in shaders, just as in other areas of programming. Blur algorithms can affect rendering speed, so the WPF BlurEffect provides the RenderingBias property as a means to choose performance or quality output for the effect. To get better quality output, alter the property as shown in Example 4-2.

DropShadowEffect

The UI design community has a turbulent relationship with the drop shadow. One decade, it's a beloved tool in UI design and it pervades the popular design metaphors, and the next it isn't. Designers are restless and inquisitive and eventually the drop shadow falls from favor and is viewed as an anachronism by the same community. If you long to add a shadowy aspect to your UI, reach for the `DropShadowEffect` class.

The Silverlight version contains a few properties that are self-explanatory (`Color`, `Opacity`, and `ShadowDepth`) so I won't burden you with a description. The `Direction` property represents the angled direction of the shadow. A direction of zero draws a shadow to the right of the host element. Higher values rotate the shadow counter-clockwise with the default value (315) placing the shadow in the lower right position. The `BlurRadius` property configures the blurriness of the shadow. Set the `BlurRadius` to zero and the shadow has a crisp, sharp edge; crank up the value for maximum shadow fuzziness.

WPF adds one additional property, `RenderingBias`, over the Silverlight version, which provides the same services as seen in the `BlurEffect.RenderingBias` property described earlier.

Nested Effects

When an effect is applied to a framework element, it affects that element and all of its children. In many circumstances, this is the appropriate approach and the UI looks as expected. Other times, the nested effects give an undesirable look to the UI. Figure 4-2 shows two stack panels with a drop shadow applied. The first stack panel has the desired look because its background brush is fully opaque. The second stack panel uses a solid color background brush with the alpha channel set to a non-opaque value. Because the brush is semi-transparent, the drop shadows for the child elements are visible.

 Take heed: once an effect is set on a parent element, there is no way to disable the effect on its children elements.

Multiple Effects on One Element

On a sophisticated interface, there might be effects applied at different levels of the visual tree. It's likely that at some point you will want to apply multiple effects to a single element. The `Effect` property has some limitations, which you should understand before proceeding. The primary constraint on your creativity is that the `Effect` property can only have a single effect in scope at any time. In other words, there is no collection of effects permitted on a `UIElement`.

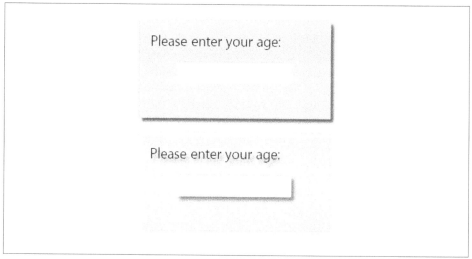

Figure 4-2. Two StackPanels with dropshadow

Imagine that you want to apply a blur and drop shadow to a button. The workaround for the single effect problem is to nest the button inside another element and apply the second effect to the containing element. Example 4-3 shows some XAML that demonstrates this technique.

Example 4-3. Using a canvas to add second effect to a button

```
<Canvas>
  <Canvas.Effect>
    <DropShadowEffect />
  </Canvas.Effect>
  <Button Content='Blurred and Shadowed'
          Width='180'
          Height='50'>
    <Button.Effect>
      <BlurEffect />
    </Button.Effect>
  </Button>
</Canvas>
```

It's a bit underwhelming to learn that Microsoft only includes these two simple effects in the framework. With the vast number of shaders known to the graphics programming crowd, I was expecting a lot more out of the box. Fortunately, Expression Blend fills in the gaps and provides many supplementary effects.

Expression Blend Effects

The Expression Blend team is constantly looking for tools to enhance the XAML design experience. A few years ago, they decided to cherry-pick the best shader effects and package them for use in Silverlight/WPF projects (see Figure 4-3). In the Blend interface, you can easily add these effects to elements via the Assets panel. You are not limited to using Expression Blend to access them, as you can always add a reference to the `Micro soft.Expression.Effects` DLL to bring them into any XAML project.

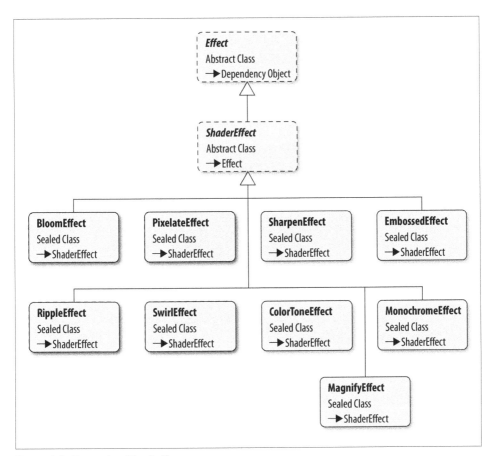

Figure 4-3. Expression Blend effects

Using a Blend Effect

The first step to using a Blend effect is to add a reference to the Blend effect library (*Microsoft.Expression.Effects.dll*). If you have installed Expression Blend in the default location, the Silverlight DLL is in the *C:\Program Files\Microsoft SDKs\Expression \Blend\Silverlight\v4.0\Libraries* directory and the WPF version is in the *C:\Program Files\Microsoft SDKs\Expression\Blend\.NETFramework\v4.0\Libraries* directory.

To use the effect in an XAML file, add the Blend namespace as shown in the following XAML (Example 4-4).

Example 4-4. Add Blend effects namespace to XAML file

```
<UserControl
  x:Class="Demo.Examples.UseBlendEffectPage"
  xmlns="http://schemas.microsoft.com/winfx/2006/xaml/presentation"
  xmlns:x="http://schemas.microsoft.com/winfx/2006/xaml"
  xmlns:ee="http://schemas.microsoft.com/expression/2010/effects"
...
```

Now it's just a matter of setting the `Effect` property and configuring some parameters, as shown here in Figure 4-4.

Figure 4-4. Using a Blend effect in the Visual Studio XAML editor

There are about a dozen standard effects in the Blend library. Blend also includes specialized effects known as transition effects. I won't detail either type of effect in this chapter, but you will see more of the standard and transition effects in Chapter 5.

You may encounter the `BitmapEffect` class and its derived types (`Bevel Bitmapeffect`, `BlurBitmapEffect`, `DropShadowBitmapEffect`, `EmbossBit mapEffect`, and `OuterGlowBitmapEffect`) while exploring the WPF libraries. Don't be fooled by the name, these are legacy effects from the early days of WPF; they are not implemented with pixel shaders. They are slow and inefficient when compared to their speedy ShaderEffect relatives and are ultimately destined for the .NET dustbin.

Custom Effects

The process of creating a custom effect starts by creating an unmanaged pixel shader. As you may recall, pixel shaders are written in their own quirky programming language called HLSL. Once the HLSL shader code is finished, it is compiled into a binary *.ps* file. To use the shader, it has to be loaded into the rendering engine input stream. To accomplish this task, you need to work with the .NET `ShaderEffect` and `PixelShader` classes.

The `ShaderEffect` is the abstract class that serves as a base for your custom effect class. It is a dependency object, so you can populate it with dependency properties. It works in conjunction with the `PixelShader` class. The `PixelShader` class is a managed wrapper around your HLSL pixel shader. Internally, the `ShaderEffect` keeps a reference to the `PixelShader` class, so that it can inject the unmanaged shader into the graphics pipeline. You will have little interaction with the `PixelShader` class, other than configuring it to load the shader. Most of the customization of your effect revolves around the `Shader Effect` class.

The `ShaderEffect` offers a handful of members that we'll examine in this chapter.

- RegisterPixelShaderSamplerProperty
- UpdateShaderValue
- PixelShaderSamplerCallback
- PixelShaderConstantCallback
- Padding

Creating a Custom ShaderEffect

Consider the following code definition:

```
public class BareBones : ShaderEffect {}
```

While this might technically be considered a `ShaderEffect`, it is an empty shell, incapable of influencing any pixels. The first step in turning the class into a useful effect is to load an unmanaged pixel shader file.

This chapter concentrates on understanding the .NET code and leaves the in-depth discussion of unmanaged pixel shaders for another chapter. To that end, the examples in this section assume that a pixel shader has been compiled into a *.ps* file and is ready to use in the custom effect.

Loading the *.ps* file

The compiled pixel shader is stored inside a binary file. It is common to name this file with a *.ps* extension, but that is not a requirement. To make it accessible to your ShaderEffect, add it to your .NET project and mark it as a project resource. It's still not usable until your ShaderEffect extracts the *.ps* file and associates it with the managed PixelShader class. The syntax for locating the *.ps* file is the same as retrieving any other project resource file. Here is some sample code (see Example 4-5) demonstrating how to extract the resource.

Example 4-5. Extracting the .ps file and assigning to PixelShader

```
public class LoadingPsFileEffect : ShaderEffect {

  public LoadingPsFileEffect() {

    // the PixelShader class provides a
    // managed wrapper for the unmanaged pixel shader
    var pixelShader = new PixelShader();

    // retrieve the .ps resource with a URI
    // the .ps file needs to be marked as resource in Build Action

    var psFileUri = new Uri
      ("/CustomShaderEffects;component/PsFiles/BlueTintEffect.ps",
        UriKind.Relative);

    pixelShader.UriSource = psFileUri;

    // store the reference to the PixelShader instance
    // in the ShaderEffect.PixelShader property
    this.PixelShader = pixelShader;
  }
}
```

The code starts by creating an instance of the PixelShader class in the class constructor. Next, a new URI is created and assigned to the PixelShader.UriSource. This example assumes that the assembly containing the resource is named CustomShaderEffects and that the *.ps* file is in the PsFiles project folder. Finally, the PixelShader reference is assigned to the ShaderEffect PixelShader property. From this point forward, the ShaderEffect will manage the communication with the GPU.

For simplicity's sake, I'll use the term GPU in this chapter to refer to both the WPF and Silverlight rendering engine. The purists in the audience will be offended but it makes it easier to talk about the process in this chapter.

The LoadingPsFileEffect class is a functional effect, so let's see how to use it in an XAML page.

Using the ShaderEffect

Using your custom effect is similar to working with the Blend effects. Start by compiling your project and then adding a custom xmlns namespace to the XAML file. This xmlns attribute indicates which assembly contains the preferred effect. Once you have the xmlns namespace configured, you can use it as the following code reveals (Example 4-6).

Example 4-6. Using the effect on an Image element

```
...
<!-- In the root element add this namespace-->
  xmlns:effects='clr-namespace:HLSL.Book.Ch04.TheEffects'

<!-- Use the Effect in your application-->
<Image Source='/Images/garden1.jpg'>
  <Image.Effect>
    <effects:LoadingPsFileEffect />
  </Image.Effect>
</Image>
...
```

Once the project is compiled, you can see the effect result by running the application or viewing it in the Visual Studio designer as shown in Figure 4-5.

Working with Samplers

In the preceding example, the ShaderEffect was applied to the entire image. Clearly, that implies that the pixels from the Image element are passed to the HLSL shader. How does that happen?

To understand how this works, we need to look at the sampler2D concept in the HLSL specification and the ShaderEffect.RegisterPixelShaderSamplerProperty in the managed libraries.

Let's start by examining the HLSL (Example 4-7) for the BlueTintEffect:

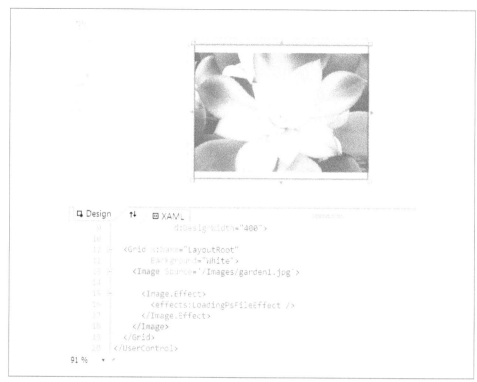

Figure 4-5. Viewing the custom effect in Visual Studio designer

Example 4-7. HLSL code for a blue tint shader

```
sampler2D input : register(s0);
float4 main(float2 uv : TEXCOORD) : COLOR  {

  float4 Color;
  Color = tex2D( input , uv.xy);
  Color.b += 1 + uv.y;
  return Color;
}
```

It's a simple color alteration shader. It applies a slight blue tint to each inbound pixel. Direct your attention to the first line of the example. It's in that first line that you see how the HLSL code gets the inbound pixels.

The HLSL specification states that pixel shaders have access to bitmap information via samplers. A *sampler* is a bitmap that is stored in video memory. In the early days of shaders, the sampler was often used to store a small texture file (for example, an image containing bricks, stones, moss, or cloth) that was mapped or painted onto a 3D object to make the model look realistic. The early graphics pioneers called it a sampler because it was a way to sample a texturemap within the shader. The terminology persists to this day. In an XAML application, the HLSL sampler usually contains the rasterized output of the effected UI elements.

Samplers are passed into the HLSL program by means of the GPU registers. To do this in HLSL, you declare a program level variable and associate it with a shader register as shown here:

```
sampler2D input : register(s0);
```

In this example, the variable name is `input` and the associated shader register is `s0`. The `sampler2D` variable type signals that the accompanying GPU register contains bitmap data.

 Samplers and other inputs to the shader are declared at the top of the HLSL code and are considered global variables by the HLSL specification. Be aware that the shader term *global variable* has a different connotation here, especially when compared to your favorite .NET language. Global variables are settable during the shader initialization phase, but cannot be changed during the shader execution. This guarantees that the parameter value is constant for all the pixels processed by the shader.

The Pixel Shader 2.0 specification permits up to 16 shader registers. Unfortunately, .NET restricts the number of accessible sampler registers to a smaller number. Silverlight and WPF 3.5 limit you to a maximum of four inputs, while WPF 4.0 is more generous and ups the input limit to eight.

Implicit input from ShaderEffect

We've just seen that the HLSL shader uses the sampler2D type for its texture input. That won't work on the .NET side; we need a Silverlight/WPF-specific type instead. The good news is that .NET uses the familiar `Brush` type for this purpose. Several types of XAML brushes can be used as input but we'll start by looking at a special, effect-friendly one called `ImplicitInputBrush`.

Example 4-8 shows one of the most common scenarios for using an effect by setting the `Effect` property on an element.

Example 4-8. Use the ImplicitInput brush

```
<TextBox>
  <!-- Use the ImplicitInput brush feature of the Effect base class -->
  <TextBox.Effect>
    <effects:BlueTintEffect />
  </TextBox.Effect>
</TextBox>
```

In this circumstance, the "sampler" that the shader gets as input is the rasterization of the `Textbox`. As mentioned above, a brush is used to send the information to the shader.

A close inspection of the XAML in Example 4-8 reveals no trace of a brush, however. What's happening?

The `ShaderEffect` base class has some default behavior that creates a special `ImplicitInputBrush` in this situation. This implicit brush contains the rasterized `Text` box pixels, which are eventually sent over to the shader for processing.

To take advantage of this implicit brush feature requires nothing more than registering the shader *.ps* file as you saw in Example 4-5. To assign any other type of brush to the shader texture requires creating an explicit `DependencyProperty` in your custom effect.

Explicit input from ShaderEffect

Start by creating a dependency property within the custom `ShaderEffect` and marking the property type as `System.Windows.Media.Brush`. Traditionally this property is named Input, but the choice of name is entirely up to you and your imagination. To integrate this Input property with the HLSL shader, you must associate the dependency property with the correct GPU **s** register. For convenience, the `ShaderEffect` class exposes the static `RegisterPixelShaderSamplerProperty` method for this purpose.

Here is the explicit way to achieve the association (Example 4-9):

Example 4-9. Writing a DependencyProperty that uses the "s" register

```
// the last argument (0) refers to the HLSL s register

public static readonly DependencyProperty InputProperty =
    ShaderEffect.RegisterPixelShaderSamplerProperty("Input",
    typeof(AddingInputTextureEffect), 0);
```

With this dependency property in place, the custom effect is applied to any brush assigned to the Input property.

Even though the effect has an explicit Input property, you can still use the syntax shown in Example 4-8 to apply the implicit brush.

At this point in the story, you know how to create an explicit input property. I'll show you how to assign other brushes to it, but first let's look at a small scenario that highlights shader input and output within the visual tree.

Pipeline trivia

To explore these concepts, I'll use a sample UI with four elements placed inside a Canvas panel. Look at the screenshot of the sample elements in the Visual Studio designer (Figure 4-6).

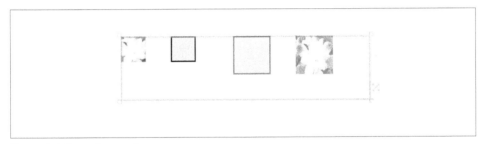

Figure 4-6. Four elements in a canvas

The first two elements on the left side have no effects configured. As you can see from the following XAML snippet (Example 4-10), there is nothing especially notable about these two elements.

Example 4-10. Two elements

```
...
<!-- Normal Image.
     Drawn at Location(0,0) Size(40,40) -->

<Image Source='/Images/garden1.jpg'
       x:Name='GardenImage'
       Width='40'
       Height='40'
       Canvas.Top='0'
       Canvas.Left='0'
       Stretch="UniformToFill" />

<!-- Normal Rectangle.
     Drawn at Location(0,80) Size(40,40) -->
<Rectangle x:Name='RectangleWithoutEffect'
           Fill='Orange'
           Width='40'
           Height='40'
           Stroke='Black'
           StrokeThickness='2'
           Canvas.Top='0'
           Canvas.Left='80' />
...
```

Silverlight/WPF processes these two elements (`GardenImage` and `RectangleWithoutEffect`) during the layout phase. Once that phase is finished, it knows the location and size for both elements and rasterizes their UI for consumption by the rendering engine.

It's a similar process for elements with effects. Take, for example, the two rectangles defined in the following XAML snippet (Example 4-11). They are similar to the prior example, but have the distinction of having the `BlueTintEffect` applied.

Example 4-11. Two rectangles with effects applied

```
...
<!-- Rectangle with Effect applied. Output from pixel shader
     is drawn at Location(0,180) Size(60,60)
     Raster input into the pixel shader comes from the Rectangle -->
<Rectangle x:Name='RectangleWithEffect1'
           Fill='Orange'
           Width='60'
           Height='60'
           Stroke='Black'
           StrokeThickness='2'
           Canvas.Top='0'
           Canvas.Left='180'>
  <Rectangle.Effect>
    <effects:BlueTintEffect />
  </Rectangle.Effect>
</Rectangle>

<!-- Rectangle with Effect applied. Output from pixel shader
     is drawn at Location(0,280) Size(60,60)
     Raster input into the pixel shader comes from the ImageBrush -->
<Rectangle x:Name='RectangleWithEffect2'
           Fill='Orange'
           Width='60'
           Height='60'
           Stroke='Black'
           StrokeThickness='2'
           Canvas.Top='0'
           Canvas.Left='280'>
  <Rectangle.Effect>
    <effects:BlueTintEffect>
      <effects:BlueTintEffect.Input>
        <ImageBrush ImageSource='{Binding
          ElementName= GardenImage,Path=Source}' />
      </effects:BlueTintEffect.Input>
    </effects:BlueTintEffect>
  </Rectangle.Effect>
</Rectangle>
...
```

Once Silverlight/WPF has finished the layout pass, it knows the location and size for `RectangleWithEffect1` and `RectangleWithEffect2`. During the rasterization phase, it passes the rasterized output data into the elements associated shader. The pixel shader does its pixel voodoo and the resultant output is placed in the regions reserved for these two rectangles.

To hammer home the point: `RectangleWithEffect1` is drawn at the same location and size regardless of whether it has an effect or not.

Explicit input revisited

So where do the inbound pixels for the pixel shader come from? That depends on a few factors. `BlueTintEffect` has an Input `DependencyProperty` defined as seen previously in Example 4-9.

Let's apply the effect and dissect where the input comes from. Example 4-12 shows the `BlueTintEffect` applied to a `Rectangle`.

Example 4-12. Using the BlueTintEffect on a Rectangle element

```
<Rectangle.Effect>
  <effects:BlueTintEffect />
</Rectangle.Effect>
```

Even though the effect has an explicit input property, it is not used when using this syntax; instead, it uses the implicit input. You can verify that this is true by checking the Input property as seen in the code in Example 4-13.

Example 4-13. Checking explicit Input brush

```
var brush =
(RectangleWithEffect1.Effect as CustomShaderEffects.InputTestEffect).Input;

// brush is null, indicating that the Input property was not set
```

Because the `BlueTintEffect` exposes an explicit Input property, it's possible to pass in other brushes to the shader input as shown in this XAML (Example 4-14).

Example 4-14. Assigning an ImageBrush to the explicit Input property

```
  <Rectangle.Effect>
    <effects:BlueTintEffect>
      <effects:BlueTintEffect.Input>
        <ImageBrush ImageSource='{Binding
          ElementName=GardenImage,Path=Source}' />
      </effects:BlueTintEffect.Input>
    </effects:BlueTintEffect>
  </Rectangle.Effect>
```

As you can see, the pixel shader input is coming from an `ImageBrush` but you can also use a `VisualBrush`, or `BitmapCacheBrush` in the same manner.

 When an effect is applied to an element, the output of the shader is exactly the same size as the original input size. If the rectangle is 60 × 80 pixels, the output of the shader is also sized at 60 × 80 pixels. Choosing implicit or explicit input has no bearing on the output size.

The only exception to the sizing rule is when an effect uses the effect padding properties.

Multi-Input Shaders

A pixel shader can have up to 16 input samplers defined in the HLSL. WPF 4.0 limits you to 8, however.

Here is a HLSL example with two input samplers defined (Example 4-15).

Example 4-15. Pixel shader with two sampler2D inputs

```
sampler2D BaseImage: register(s0);
sampler2D TextureMap : register(s1);

float4 main(float2 uv : TEXCOORD) : COLOR
{
  float hOffset = frac(uv.x / 1 + 1);
  float vOffset = frac(uv.y / 1 + 1);
  float2 offset = tex2D(TextureMap, float2(hOffset, vOffset)).xy * 4 - 1/2;

  float4 outputColor = tex2D(BaseImage, frac(uv + offset ));
  return outputColor;
}
```

The first `sample2D` variable is using the s0 register while the second `sample2D` variable maps to the s1 register.

 Be pragmatic and thoughtful when naming your HLSL variables. Readability is just as important in HLSL code as in other programming languages.

In this example, the first sample2D variable name reflects its status as the base image. The second variable name, `TextureMap`, indicates that it holds a bitmap containing lookup textures. The HLSL in the sample uses a simple mapping technique to blend the pixels from the two sampler inputs.

On the .NET side, you need to create two dependency properties and call `ShaderEffect.RegisterPixelShaderSamplerProperty` on both. The registration code will be similar to the code shown in Example 4-9.

To use these inputs in XAML, use syntax like this (Example 4-16):

Example 4-16. Assigning some ImageBrushes to the input properties

```
...
<Rectangle x:Name='RectangleWithEffect1'
           Width='256'
           Height='170'
           Stroke='Black'
           StrokeThickness='2'>
  <Rectangle.Effect>
    <effects:TwoInputEffect>
```

```
    <effects:TwoInputEffect.BaseImage>
      <ImageBrush ImageSource='{Binding
                  ElementName=GardenImage2,Path=Source}' />
    </effects:TwoInputEffect.BaseImage>

    <effects:TwoInputEffect.TextureMap>
      <ImageBrush ImageSource='{Binding
                  ElementName=GardenImage1,Path=Source}' />
    </effects:TwoInputEffect.TextureMap>
  </effects:TwoInputEffect>

  </Rectangle.Effect>
</Rectangle>
...
```

This is a beautiful effect as you can see in the screenshot below (Figure 4-7). It shows four images, the left two being the original images and the right two showing the texture mapping.

Figure 4-7. Two original images and two blended images

Understanding Sampler Size

All sampler inputs into the shader are resized by the Silverlight/WPF runtime to match the render size of the host element.

Consider the following XAML (Example 4-17):

Example 4-17. Effect brushes with mismatched size

```
...
<Rectangle x:Name='Rectangle1'
            Width='400'
            Height='400'>
  <Rectangle.Effect>
    <effects:TwoInputEffect>

      <effects:TwoInputEffect.BaseImage>

        <!-- flowers_wide.jpg is  925 × 260 pixels -->
        <ImageBrush ImageSource='/Images/flowers_wide.jpg' />
      </effects:TwoInputEffect.BaseImage>
      <effects:TwoInputEffect.TextureMap>

        <!-- garden_small.jpg is  150 × 200 pixels -->
        <ImageBrush ImageSource='/Images/garden_small.jpg' />
      </effects:TwoInputEffect.TextureMap>
    </effects:TwoInputEffect>
  </Rectangle.Effect>
</Rectangle>
...
```

This example uses the TwoInputEffect and assigns an ImageBrush to each sampler input. During the layout pass, the runtime determines the render size and location for the host rectangle, in this case, a 400 × 400 square. When each ImageBrush is readied for the shader, its sized is constrained to the same 400 × 400 size as the host rectangle, causing the larger image to be compressed and the smaller image to be enlarged. As far as the HLSL shader is concerned, it gets two 400 × 400 textures assigned to its s registers. If you could debug the shader pipeline and look at the two textures stored in video memory, you'd see that this is true.

Use a transform to manipulate an input brush before the scaling occurs, as shown in Example 4-18:

Example 4-18. Transforming a brush before sending to shader

```
...
<effects:TwoInputEffect.TextureMap>
  <ImageBrush ImageSource='/Images/flowers_wide.jpg'>
    <ImageBrush.Transform>
      <CompositeTransform ScaleX = '.4'
                          ScaleY = '.4'
                 TranslateX = '100' />
    </ImageBrush.Transform>
  </ImageBrush>
</effects:TwoInputEffect.TextureMap>
...
```

Now that you've seen how to pass bitmap parameters to the shader, it's time to expand your horizons and see how to pass other types of parameters into the shader.

Creating Parameterized Effects

Parameters are the lifeblood of a flexible programming model. Can you imagine how dull and impractical it would be to work in a programming language without parameters? Luckily for us, HLSL accepts various types of input data into the shader.

You've already seen how to pass bitmap data to the pixel shader through the GPU registers. To be more precise, we used the sampler registers for this purpose. They are designated with the "s" nomenclature (s0, s1, s2, etc.). You are not limited to passing bitmap data into the shader as HLSL sports another set of registers known as the constant registers (c0, c1, c2, etc.). A constant parameter is similar to a readonly field in C#. The value is changeable during the pixel shader initialization period, but remains constant throughout the execution of the shader. In other words, once the value is set, it will be the same for every pixel processed by the pixel shader. You can have up to 32 constant registers in PS_2_0. PS_3_0 expands that to 224, but is only accessible in WPF 4.0.

Let's rewrite the multi-input shader as follows:

Example 4-19. Adding constant registers to the HLSL shader

```
sampler2D BaseImage: register(s0);
sampler2D TextureMap : register(s1);
float vertScale : register(c0);
float horzScale : register(c1);
float translateX : register(c30);
float translateY : register(c31);

float4 main(float2 uv : TEXCOORD): COLOR
{

  float hOffset = frac(uv.x / vertScale + translateX);
  float vOffset = frac(uv.y / horzScale + translateY);
  float2 offset = tex2D(TextureMap, float2(hOffset, vOffset)).xy * 4 - (1/2);

    float4 outputColor = tex2D(BaseImage, frac(uv + offset ));
    return outputColor;
}
```

In addition to the sampler2D inputs shown earlier in Example 4-15, the refactored code contains four additional input values declared at the top of the pixel shader. If you look closely, you can see that these new items are float values, which are loaded into registers c0, c1, c30 and c31, and then used inside the main function.

The ShaderEffect class transmits parameter information to an HLSL constant register through a DependencyProperty. It does this by using the special PixelShaderConstant Callback method. The trip is one-way, from the effect class to the pixel shader. The parameter value never travels back to the effect class.

Now, let's focus on how to write the effect to take advantage of these parameters. Here is a snippet (Example 4-20) that shows the DependencyProperty registration:

Example 4-20. Binding the "c" registers with PixelShaderConstantCallback

```
...
public static readonly DependencyProperty VertScaleProperty =
  DependencyProperty.Register("VerticalScale", typeof(double),
    typeof(InputParametersEffect),
      new PropertyMetadata(((double)(0D)),
        PixelShaderConstantCallback(0)));

public static readonly DependencyProperty HorzScaleProperty =
  DependencyProperty.Register("HorizontalScale", typeof(double),
    typeof(InputParametersEffect),
      new PropertyMetadata(((double)(0D)),
        PixelShaderConstantCallback(1)));

// ... continue in this manner for other dependency properties
```

The last argument on each registration line is the important one for this discussion. We call the PixelShaderConstantCallback method and pass in the appropriate constant register. PixelShaderConstantCallback sets up a PropertyChangedCallback delegate, which is invoked whenever the DependencyProperty is changed. Example 4-21 shows how easy it is to use these new properties.

Example 4-21. Setting some shader parameters via DependencyProperties

```
...
<Rectangle x:Name='RectangleWithEffect2'
            Width='Auto'
            Height='Auto'
            Margin='3'
            Grid.Row='1'>
<Rectangle.Effect>
  <effects:InputParametersEffect
        HorizontalScale='{Binding ElementName= horzSlider, Path=Value}'
        VerticalScale='{Binding ElementName=vertSlider, Path=Value}'
        TranslateX='{Binding ElementName=xSlider,Path=Value}'
        TranslateY='{Binding ElementName=ySlider,Path=Value}'>

    <effects:InputParametersEffect.BaseImage>
      <ImageBrush ImageSource='/Images/Garden1.jpg' />
    </effects:InputParametersEffect.BaseImage>

    <effects:InputParametersEffect.TextureMap>
      <ImageBrush ImageSource='/Images/Garden2.jpg' />
    </effects:InputParametersEffect.TextureMap>
  </effects:InputParametersEffect>
</Rectangle.Effect>
</Rectangle>
...
```

UpdateShaderValue

There is one more step necessary to make a functional ShaderEffect. You need to invoke the UpdateShaderValue method in the class constructor for every bound Dependency

Property; otherwise, the pixel shader won't be initialized with the default values for the property. Call the method for every effect property, as shown in Example 4-22, to ensure that the initial value for each property is set in the pixel shader.

Example 4-22. Using the UpdateShaderValue method in the effect constructor

```
this.UpdateShaderValue(InputProperty);
this.UpdateShaderValue(TextureMapProperty);
this.UpdateShaderValue(VerticalScaleProperty);
this.UpdateShaderValue(HorizontalScaleProperty);
```

Property Types

On the HLSL side, the constant register works with various types of float values. When you register a `ShaderEffect` `DependencyProperty` with the `PixelShaderConstantCall` back method, you are limited to a short list of .NET types. Table 4-1 lists the permitted .NET types, and the matching HLSL types.

Table 4-1. Comparing WPF, Silverlight, and HLSL property types

WPF	Silverlight	HLSL
Single	Single	float
Double	Double	float
Point	Point	float2
Size	Size	float2
Color	Color	float4
Vector	NA	float2
Point3D	NA	float3
Vector3D	NA	float3
Point4D	NA	float4

Padding

Normally, an effect is applied to an element's actual render size. Therefore an effect for a 200 × 200 Image will modify pixels in a 200 × 200 region. Certain effects, like the drop shadow, need additional space outside the normal render area. Use the `ShaderEffect` padding properties (`PaddingTop`, `PaddingLeft`, `PaddingRight`, `PaddingBottom`) to increase the size passed into the pixel shader.

The padding properties are marked as protected scope, so you cannot access them outside your `ShaderEffect`. The typical pattern is to set the padding within your type and expose other dependency properties for client code to access. The built-in `DropShadowEffect` uses the `ShadowDepthProperty` in this manner.

Effect Mapping

Distortion effects are a popular use of pixel shaders (see Figure 4-8).

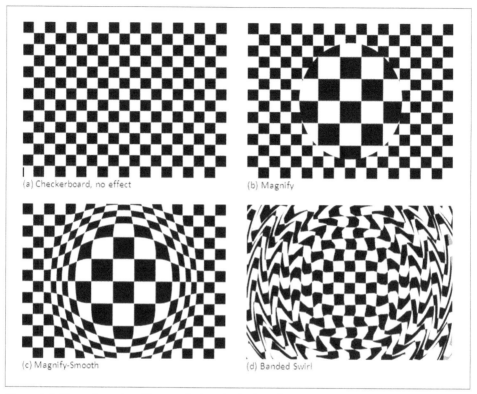

(a) Checkerboard, no effect

(b) Magnify

(c) Magnify-Smooth

(d) Banded Swirl

Figure 4-8. Three distortion effects applied to checkerboard.

Distortion effects require extra work if you want them to behave in a predictable fashion. When you apply a distortion effect to an interactive element like a list box (Figure 4-9.a), the touch, stylus, and mouse events won't work as expected. The pixel shader is rearranging the output pixels, but the Silverlight/WPF hit-testing infrastructure is unaware that the pixels are in a new location (Figure 4-9.b).

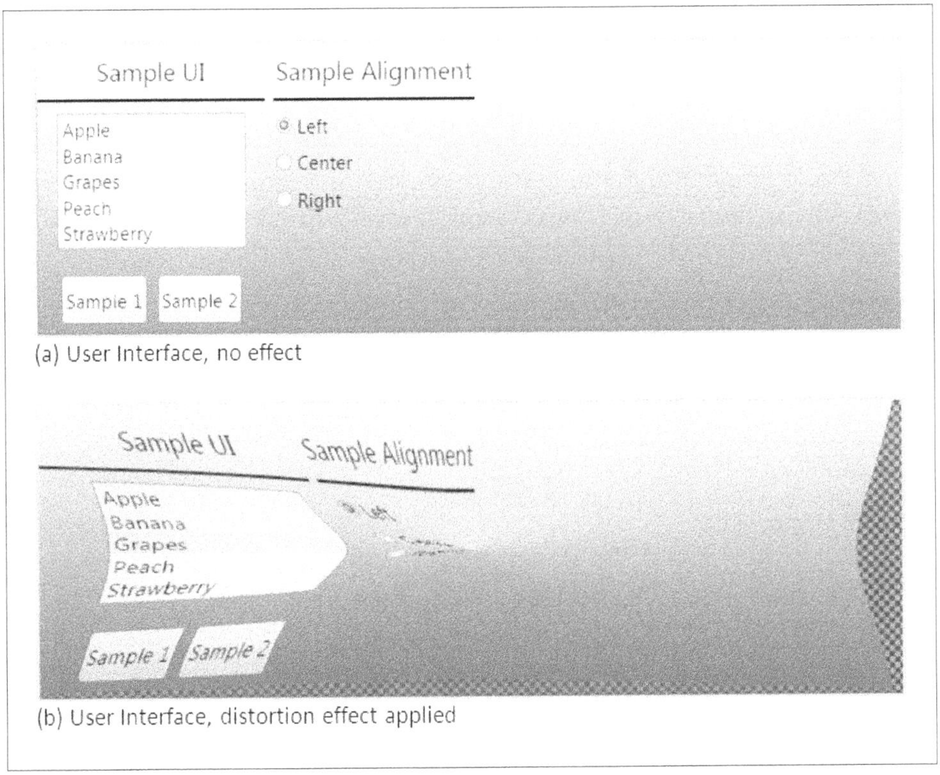

(a) User Interface, no effect

(b) User Interface, distortion effect applied

Figure 4-9. UI with Distortion Effect

The EffectMapping property provides a way to synchronize the input coordinates between the two worlds. It takes the raw input coordinates and maps them to the pixel shader coordinates. This is accomplished by creating a custom GeneralTransform class.

Before we examine the customized GeneralTransform, let's look at the sample compression shader (Example 4-23) that lives on the HLSL side.

Example 4-23. A compression shader

```
sampler2D input : register(s0);
float CrushFactor : register(c0);

float4 main(float2 uv : TEXCOORD) : COLOR
{

  if (uv.y >= CrushFactor )
  {
    float crushAmount = lerp(0, 1, (uv.y - CrushFactor)/(1 - CrushFactor));
    float2 pos = float2(uv.x, crushAmount );
    return tex2D(input, pos);
  }
```

```
    else return float4(0,0,0,0);
}
```

This HLSL example takes the incoming pixels and compresses the pixel shader output toward the bottom of the element. The higher the CrushFactor property value, the shorter the output image will be.

In the XAML snippet shown below (Example 4-24), the CrushEffect causes the Image to be rendered at 30% of its original height.

Example 4-24. Applying the CrushEffect

```
...
<Border BorderBrush='Red'
        BorderThickness='4'
        Width='240'
        Height='120'
        Margin='5'
        Grid.Row='2'>
  <Image  Stretch='Fill'
          Source='/Images/garden1.jpg'
          MouseMove='distortedImage2_MouseMove'
          MouseLeftButtonUp='distortedImage2_MouseLeftButtonUp'
          Name='distortedImage2'>
    <Image.Effect>
      <effects:CrushWithMappingEffect CrushFactor='.7'/>
    </Image.Effect>
  </Image>
</Border>
...
```

Figure 4-10 shows the output of the CrushEffect, when applied to an Image element. The image is wrapped in a Border element, which shows the size of the Image if it didn't have the effect applied.

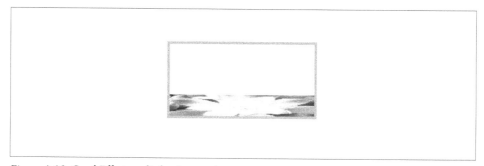

Figure 4-10. CrushEffect applied to Image element

If there is no EffectMapping provided, the image mouse events will fire when the mouse is within the white area, even though it's evident in the screenshot that the image pixels are no longer visible in that region. To fix this shortcoming, create an EffectMapping property. The `ImageMapping` property is responsible for returning a custom `General Transform` class to the Silverlight/WPF engine as seen in this code scrap.

Example 4-25. Creating an EffectMapping property

```
private CrushTransform _transform = new CrushTransform();
protected override GeneralTransform EffectMapping {
  get {

    _transform.CrushFactor = CrushFactor;

    return _transform;
  }
}
```

GeneralTransform class

The `GeneralTransform` class is one of the XAML transform classes. Though not as familiar as other transforms like `CompositeTransform`, it is used by the framework during certain transform actions like `TransformToVisual` and `EffectMapping`. It contains a few members of interest. It has two transform methods, `Transform` and `TryTransform`. Both methods take an incoming point and return a transformed point. The difference between the two is that the `TryTransform` method returns a `Boolean`, instead of throwing an exception if the transform fails for any reason, and it uses an out parameter to deliver the transformed point back to the caller. Example 4-26 shows a few of the members of the `GeneralTransform` class.

Example 4-26. Prototyping the GeneralTransform class

```
public class GeneralTransform
{
  // a few of the class members
  public Point Transform(Point point) {
    Point point1;
    if (this.TryTransform(point, out point1)) {
      return point1;
    }
    else {
      throw new InvalidOperationException("Could not transform");
    }}

public abstract bool TryTransform(Point inPoint, out Point outPoint);
}
// sub-classing the GeneralTransform class
public class SampleTransform : GeneralTransform {}
```

Were you to create an instance of the `SampleTransform` class shown in Example 4-26, you could easily get a transformed point with code similar to (Example 4-27).

Example 4-27. Getting a transformed point

```
var transform = new SampleTransform();
var originalPoint = new Point(10, 20);
Point transformedPoint;

if (transform.TryTransform(originalPoint, out transformedPoint)) {
  // do something with the out parameter
  Console.WriteLine(transformedPoint.Y);
}
```

The `GeneralTransform` class also has an `Inverse` property. This property is utilized whenever an inverted version of the transform is needed, and it is this property that is called during the effect mapping operations. It returns a reference to another transform, as shown in Example 4-28.

Example 4-28. Getting the inverse transform from the general transform class

```
var t1 = new CrushTransform();
var t2 = crushTransform.Inverse as InverseCrushTransform;
```

GeneralTransform and EffectMapping property

The `ShaderEffect` `EffectMapping` property tells the Silverlight/WPF framework which `GeneralTransform` class to use during hit-testing and other input events. The framework follows this workflow. When a mouse event is detected (mousemove), the framework get the transform from the `EffectMapping` property. Next, it calls the `Inverse` method to get the undo transform. Finally, it calls the `TryTransform` method on the inverted transform to get the corrected mouse location.

For every distortion action in the pixel shader, you provide an undo action in the `Inverse` transformation class. For intricate shaders, the transformation code can get quite complex. The different algorithms available in the HLSL and .NET frameworks exacerbate the problem. Nevertheless, it is your responsibility to write the transform to make hit testing work correctly.

Here is some code (Example 4-29) that demonstrates the transforms that reverse the `CrushEffect`.

Example 4-29. General and Inverse transforms

```
public class CrushTransform : GeneralTransform
{
  // create a DependencyProperty that matches the DependencyProperty
  // in the CrushEffect ShaderEffect class.
  // Is used to pass information from the ShaderEffect to the Transform
  public static readonly DependencyProperty CrushFactorProperty =
    DependencyProperty.Register("CrushFactor", typeof(double),
    typeof(CrushTransform),
    new PropertyMetadata(new double()));

  public double CrushFactor {
```

```
      get { return (double)GetValue(CrushFactorProperty); }
      set { SetValue(CrushFactorProperty, value); }
    }
    protected bool IsTransformAvailable(Point inPoint) {
      if (inPoint.Y < CrushFactor) {
        return false; // No transform available for this point location
      }
      else {
        return true;
      }
    }
    public override bool TryTransform(Point inPoint, out Point outPoint) {
      outPoint = new Point();

      // normal transform actions
      double ratio = inPoint.X;
      outPoint.Y = CrushFactor + (1 - CrushFactor) * ratio;
      outPoint.X = inPoint.X;

      return IsTransformAvailable(inPoint);
    }

    public override GeneralTransform Inverse {
      get {
        // this method is called by framework
        // when it needs an inverse version of the transform
        return new InverseCrushTransform { CrushFactor = CrushFactor };
      }
    }

    public override Rect TransformBounds(Rect rect) {
      throw new NotImplementedException();
    }
  }
  public class InverseCrushTransform : CrushTransform
  {
    public override bool TryTransform(Point inPoint, out Point outPoint) {
      outPoint = new Point();

      // inverse transform actions
      double ratio = (inPoint.Y - CrushFactor) / (1 - CrushFactor);
      outPoint.Y = inPoint.Y * ratio;
      outPoint.X = inPoint.X;
      return base.IsTransformAvailable(inPoint);
    }
  }
}
```

Summary

Silverlight/WPF has a nice system for integrating shaders and .NET effects. This chapter showed you how to make the managed wrapper for the HLSL shader.

Let's review the steps needed to create your own shaders.

- Write a shader in HLSL.
- Compile the shader to a binary file (.ps) with *FXC.exe* or another HLSL compiler.
- Add the .ps file to your Silverlight/WPF project and set the build action to `Resource`.
- Create a .NET effect class that derives from `ShaderEffect`.
- Load the .ps file into the effect class and assign it to the class's `PixelShader` property.
- Set up one or more input dependency properties of type `Brush` and use the `ShaderEffect.RegisterPixelShaderSamplerProperty` method to map the input to the correct GPU `s` register.
- If the shader has parameters, map each parameter to a dependency property and bind to the correct GPU `c` register with the `PixelShaderConstantCallback` method.
- In the effect constructor, call `UpdateShaderValue` for each `DependencyProperty` in the class.
- For certain shader types, create Padding or EffectMapping code.
- Apply the effect to any `UIElement`.

 The WPF and Silverlight teams took different routes when creating the ShaderEffect and PixelShader classes. Looking at the public interfaces of the implementation, the classes look nearly identical, but a quick look at the internal implementation shows some differences. If you plan on creating shaders that work in both systems, be cognizant of the potential internal differences and test accordingly.

As you've seen in this chapter, there are many steps necessary to create a working shader effect class. To ease the development of custom shaders, I created a specialized utility called Shazzam Shader Editor. It automates most of the steps needed to make effects. A detailed tour of Shazzam is imminent, but first comes a chapter showing how to use Expression Blend to add effects to any Silverlight/WPF project.

CHAPTER 5

Using Expression Blend and Visual Studio with Shaders

Visual Studio, boasts a rock-solid XAML text editor, which makes it a perfect tool for code hackers and other hardcore UI developers, people who revel in writing interfaces one markup element at a time.

Expression Blend, on the other hand, enables the visualizers of the world, the designers and integrators on your team, to take their mental blueprints and coerce them into reality, one pixel at a time. Sadly, Blend is still relatively unknown and underutilized by XAML developers and designers alike. But I'm doing my part; you'll see some of its design-centric tools in this chapter.

The truth, at least as I see it, is that both tools are essential for a well-balanced approach to XAML editing and design. There are times when it's best to leave Visual Studio and use Blend and other moments where it's best to work in Visual Studio. Microsoft is melding the two tools together in a future version of Visual Studio, which could mean that the switch is no longer necessary, but that combined nirvana is still some months in the future.

The objective of this chapter is to show the effect-specific tools offered in these indispensable XAML editors. It starts on the Blend side, showing the basic design tools and editors, and then examines the transition effects available in the Blend Visual State Manager. Interwoven amidst the Blend topics are a few excursions to the Visual Studio side of the house to learn where it outshines the Blend tooling.

Creating a Project

Here's the plan for the projects in the chapter. We'll create a new Blend project and add some existing images and custom shaders to it. Next, we'll use the images, adding them to the designer and use the Blend Assets panel to assign some effects to the image.

Along the way, you'll see how to use the Properties panel to edit the effect properties and how to designate multiple inputs for an effect.

New Project

Start by opening Expression Blend on your computer. The examples in this chapter are using Blend 4 but newer versions should behave in a similar fashion.

You should see a start screen similar to Figure 5-1.

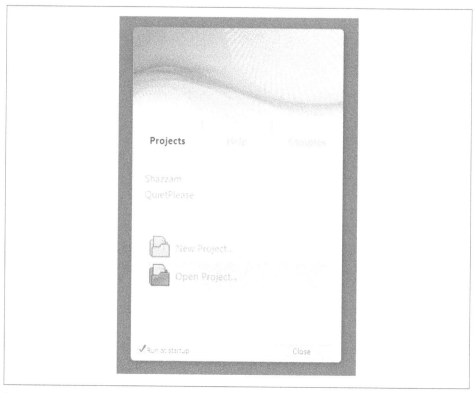

Figure 5-1. Expression Blend Start Screen

Click the New Project... button. In the New Project dialog (shown in Figure 5-2), select the WPF Project type, and then set the project name, language, and location as desired. Click OK to create the new project.

At this point, you have a new project in Blend with files and settings similar to new projects created with Visual Studio. If you need confirmation of the similarity, spend a few minutes exploring the Project panel before continuing.

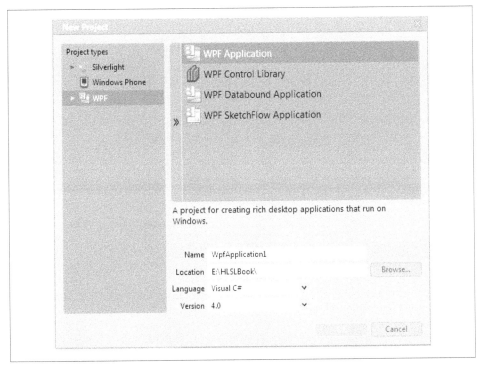

Figure 5-2. New project dialog in Expression Blend

In the center of the work-area is a white rectangular drawing surface known as the *Artboard*. It is here that all the design magic happens in Expression Blend. Let's start simply, by adding some assets to the project and drawing an image on the Artboard.

Adding Assets

Right-click the project in the Projects panel, choose the Add Existing Item... context menu and add a few image files to the project (Figure 5-3).

 In the companion code samples for this book are a number of assets, including the images and reference DLL used in this example. Feel free to use these assets or supply your own for the Blend project.

The Blend Assets panel provides an effortless way to add image files to the Artboard.

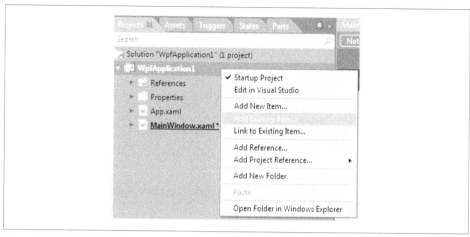

Figure 5-3. Add Existing Item... menu

Expression Blend has a highly customizable window layout feature. It allows you to take a snapshot of a custom tools layout and save into the workspaces collection. The Workspaces menu provides a way to switch between the saved layouts.

Ensure that the Window→Workspaces→Design menu is checked before continuing.

The Assets panel should appear on the left side of the workspace. If it is not visible, open the Window menu and confirm there is a checkmark next to the Assets menu item.

Open the Assets panel and select the Media section as shown in Figure 5-4. Blend populates the Media section with pictures, videos, and other media located within your project files. Drag the image from the Assets panel to the Artboard. For large images, it might be necessary to resize the image element after is placed on the Artboard. This is achieved by dragging the sizing handles on the edges of the control. To keep the original image aspect ratio, hold down the Shift key while resizing.

Adding Effects

The Assets panel makes it just as easy to add an effect to the designer. Figure 5-5 shows the default effects loaded by Expression Blend.

Some of the effects listed are recognizable from earlier chapters (DropShadowEffect, BlurEffect). The other nine in the list are effects created by the Blend team. The sharp-eyed reader will note that there are more than nine effects, even if you discount the two built-in framework effects. All the Bloom entries really use the same effect class

Figure 5-4. Assets panel, showing the Media content and Artboard

(`BloomEffect`); each entry defaults to a unique set of property settings. You can see an example of each of the Bloom entries in Figure 5-6.

Adding an effect is almost too easy. Just drag the effect from the Assets panel and drop it on the target element. Blend immediately shows the effect in the Artboard and updates the Objects and Timeline view (See Figure 5-7) to indicate that an effect is available and configurable.

Select the effect in the Objects and Timeline panel to edit its properties. To delete the effect, select it in the panel and press the Delete key.

 The Objects and Timeline panel is usually found docked to the bottom of the Projects panel on the left side of the Blend interface.

By default, the rendering of effects on the Artboard is turned off. This a prudent choice by the Blend engineers, as it ensures that we get the maximum rendering performance while working in the Blend interface. But that doesn't help visualize the effect during design time; we want to see what the effect looks like on our visual elements. To change this setting, toggle the fx button (See Figure 5-8) located at the bottom left edge of the Artboard.

The fx button influences all the effects within the current view. To toggle an individual effect's visibility inside the Artboard, click the Eye button in the Objects and Timeline view. Look at Figure 5-7 again. On the right side of the panel is a column of eye buttons.

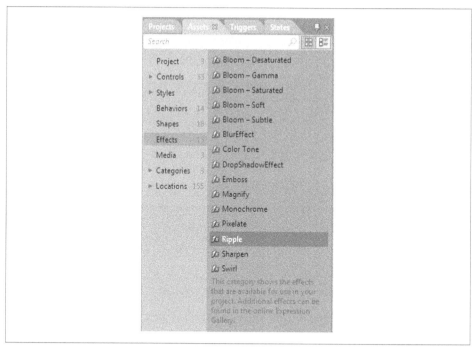

Figure 5-5. Effects section of the Assets panel

Click on the Eye button next to an effect to disable the effect for that element. Blend changes the eye icon to a dot icon to signify that the effect is off (just in case you couldn't tell by looking at the Artboard). Click on the Eye (dot) button to show the effect again.

Setting Effect Properties

Most effects have settable properties and the Properties panel gives you a visual tool for reading and setting individual properties. Figure 5-9 shows a flower image with the `RippleEffect` applied. When the effect is selected in the Objects and Timeline panel, the effect properties automatically show-up in the panel.

Modify the values in the Properties panel, and see what happens with the effect. You can also change the property setting by dragging the numeric values with your mouse pointer.

Visual Studio Editor

It's time to leave the artful confines of Blend and explore the no-nonsense tools incorporated within Visual Studio. Expression Blend and Visual Studio share the same file formats, so you can open existing projects created with either tool without any complications.

Figure 5-6. All the Bloom effect configurations

Figure 5 7. Objects and Timeline panel, showing effect

As you've seen, the Expression Blend Objects and Timeline panel provides a nice way to view a UI element and its affiliated effect. There is a similar panel in Visual Studio, called the Document Outline, but it's not visible by default. Press Ctrl-Alt-T and the Document Outline will appear. It's usually docked to the left side of Visual Studio window (Figure 5-10), located in the same general area as the Toolbox and Server Explorer windows.

Figure 5-8. Fx button on the Artboard

Figure 5-9. Editing effect properties

To change the property values, select the `RippleEffect` in the outline and edit the effect properties in the Visual Studio property grid (Figure 5-11).

There's not much more you can do with effects in Visual Studio. It does a nice job rendering the effect in the designer and it has better support for choosing alternate input brushes for multi-input shaders. But it's missing the ability to add effects to the Toolbox which eliminates the option of dragging an effect onto the Visual Studio designer surface.

Using Custom Effects in Blend

In the previous chapter, we looked at ways to add a custom effect to a Visual Studio project. There were many steps involved, importing binary *.ps* files, creating custom shader classes, and so on. In the real world, most of that work will happen in a class library project, which is then compiled to a reusable DLL file. Once the effects are compiled into the assembly, they can be added to a project like any other reference library.

Figure 5-10. The Document Outline window

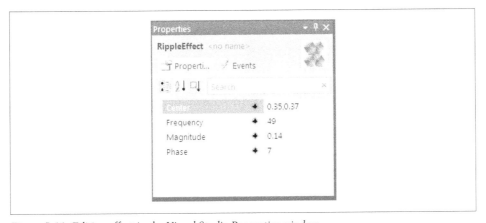

Figure 5-11. Editing effect in the Visual Studio Properties window

I suspect that most developers will add references using the familiar and well-known Visual Studio reference tools. That's not to say you can't add a reference in Blend. Choose the Project→Add Reference... menu (or Alt-Shift-R) to open a dialog and select your reference DLL.

 For the examples in this section, I am referencing the shadervault.dll file found in the code directory.

Blend inspects all referenced assemblies for classes that derive from `ShaderEffect` and adds them to the Assets panel. Figure 5-12 shows the Effects section after adding a reference to my custom `shadervault` assembly. Consequently, I can drag these custom effects over to the Artboard in the same manner as using the built-in effects.

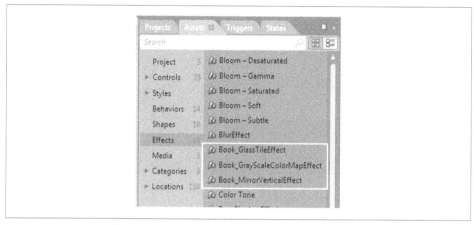

Figure 5-12. Custom effects added from referenced assembly

For the next example, I converted the angelic female face into the unsettling caricature shown in Figure 5-13 in only a few minutes. It was done with the judicious use of the `Book_MirrorVerticalEffect` and few minutes tweaking the effect properties. Try it yourself. Drag the effect to the image, and then fine-tune the properties to create your own monstrous rendition.

> I used the Book_ prefix on the effects in the shadervault library to make them easier to find in the book examples.

Multi-Input Effects

Effects occasionally have multiple inputs, so it would be nice if the Microsoft tools provided the means to select alternative brushes for the effects. Surprisingly, Visual Studio has the better tooling for this behavior.

Take this example (Example 5-1).

Example 5-1. The Book_GrayScaleColorMapEffect

```
<Image Stretch='UniformToFill'
       Width='300'
       Source='/UseShaders;component/NiceFace.jpg'>
  <Image.Effect>
```

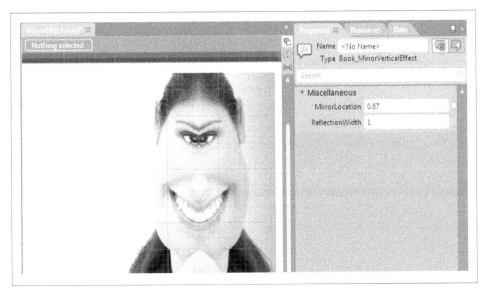

Figure 5-13. Using custom effect

```
    <effects:Book_GrayScaleColorMapEffect  BandOffset='0.4'>
    </effects:Book_GrayScaleColorMapEffect>
  </Image.Effect>
</Image>
```

This effect provides two inputs. The first property, `Input`, defines the image to change. The second property, `AlternateColorMap`, defines a color lookup texture. The effect works by changing the original colors of the Input to the lookup values supplied in the `AlternateColorMap` brush.

In the XAML shown in Example 5-1, the effect is applied to an image. The way the effect is used in this example, the Input property is assigned from the implicit input brush, meaning the input is comprised of the image pixels.

Now consider a scenario where I have a `Rectangle` element with the same effect applied. I'd like to provide two explicit brushes for the input, as shown here (Example 5-2).

Example 5-2. Rectangle and effect with two inputs

```
<Rectangle Width='Auto'
           Height=Auto>
  <Rectangle.Effect>
    <effects:Book_GrayScaleColorMapEffect>
      <effects:Book_GrayScaleColorMapEffect.Input>
        <!-- brush 1-->
      </effects:Book_GrayScaleColorMapEffect.Input>
      <effects:Book_GrayScaleColorMapEffect.AlternateColorMap>
        <!-- brush 2-->
      </effects:Book_GrayScaleColorMapEffect.AlternateColorMap>
    </effects:Book_GrayScaleColorMapEffect>
```

```
        </Rectangle.Effect>
    </Rectangle>
```

Setting brushes with Property window

Rather than typing the XAML in the text editor, I like to use the Visual Studio tools to specify the explicit brushes.

Start the process by choosing the effect (as shown in Figure 5-10) in the Visual Studio document outline window. Once the effect is selected, look at the Properties windows (press F4 if it is not visible) and you should see something similar to the following screenshot (Figure 5-14).

Figure 5-14. Properties for the Book_GrayScaleColorMapEffect class

This looks promising. Both input properties are evident in the property grid and there is a build button visible on the right side of each property. Clicking the build button opens a brush chooser (Figure 5-15).

Figure 5-15. Brush Chooser overlay

I want to use an image brush for the `AlternateColorMap` property; here are the steps necessary in the brush chooser overlay.

- Click the Build button to open the brush chooser.
- Click the Image button at the top of the chooser (the fourth button from the left).
- Click the Select Image button on the bottom right of the chooser.
- Choose an image that contains the desired color map (See Figure 5-16).

Figure 5-16. Choose Image dialog

Do the same steps for the Input property and admire the results (See Figure 5-17).

Figure 5-17. Effect with color map and input image

Transition Effects in Blend

One of my favorite features of Silverlight/WPF is the *Visual State Manager* (*VSM*). It lets you define a collection of visual looks (or *states*, as they described in the documentation) for an element. Once the visual states are ready, the VSM handles the transitions between the states. Expression Blend includes a States panel that simplifies composing and previewing the visual states. There's no equivalent tooling in Visual Studio.

You might be wondering why the VSM is appearing in this chapter. Ah, my friends, it's because you can employ an effect when switching between states.

The example is this section will use the VSM to create a mouse enter and mouse leave state.

Visualize this: an application has a small image on the screen. When the user mouses over the image, it changes state, and increases in size; when the user moves the mouse away from the image, the state changes again, with the image returning to the original size. It's a common UI tactic—we've seen website variants of this metaphor for years.

Create a State Group

Let's start with a clean slate. In my project, I'm using WPF, so I'll create a new Window item and add an image to the Artboard. To add the mouse states, open the States panel (Figure 5-18).

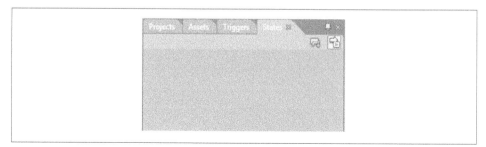

Figure 5-18. The States panel

On the top right side of the States panel is an Add State Group button. Figure 5-19 shows the new State group created by clicking on the button. As you can see in the screenshot, I've named the state group `MouseStateGroup` and provided a 1.2 second default transition time.

Figure 5-19. MouseStateGroup with 1.2-second default transition time

Add the States

If you look closely on the right side of the state group row, there is an Add State button. Click that button twice, to add two states, and name them MouseEnter and MouseLeave.

Select the MouseEnter state in the VSM and note the red border surrounding the Artboard. This slim border indicates that any changes you make in the Artboard are stored in the MouseEnter state. In case the red border isn't enough of a clue, Blend also adds the text "MouseEnter state recording is on" at the top of the Artboard. To change other State item properties, for example MouseLeave, just select the state in the State panel. Blend will store the visual state for each item separately, saving the information when changing to any other state.

You can preview the animated transitions between VSM states by switching on the Transition preview feature (Figure 5-20). When enabled, Blend shows the live animation whenever you switch states in MouseStateGroup.

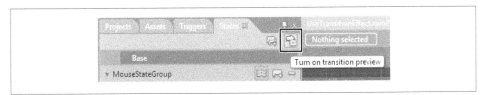

Figure 5-20. Toggle transition preview button

Set the Properties

To change the size of the image for the MouseEnter state, select the image and then find the Render Transform section of the Property panel. As you can see in Figure 5-21, I've set the ScaleTransform values to 1.25.

Now comes the fun part: watching the state transitions. Click the MouseEnter and MouseLeave entries in the State panel. You should see the size of the image grow or shrink on each click.

Figure 5-21. Setting ScaleTransform in the Property panel

 Remember, the Transition preview button must be enabled to see the animation in the Artboard.

Adding a Transition Effect

Our state changes are finished. All that's left to do is add the transition effect. Find the fx button in the State panel. It is on the same row as the Default transition setting. Clicking on the fx button (See Figure 5-22) reveals a selection of transition effects.

My favorite effects for this sample are Radial Blur and Ripple. I encourage you to experiment with the others on the list to see which ones you like.

To see the effect in action, click the MouseEnter and MouseLeave entries in the State panel.

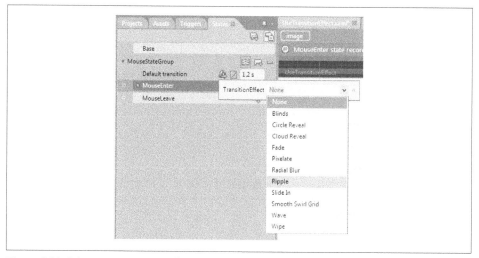

Figure 5-22. Selecting a transition effect

Transition Effect

A few words about the transition effects included in the VSM (shown in Figure 5-23). These are special purpose effects created by the Blend team especially for the VSM transitions. They are well hidden with Blend, only discoverable in the States panel and the add Effect button in the properties panel. Despite being hard to find, they are just a special kind of multi-input effect.

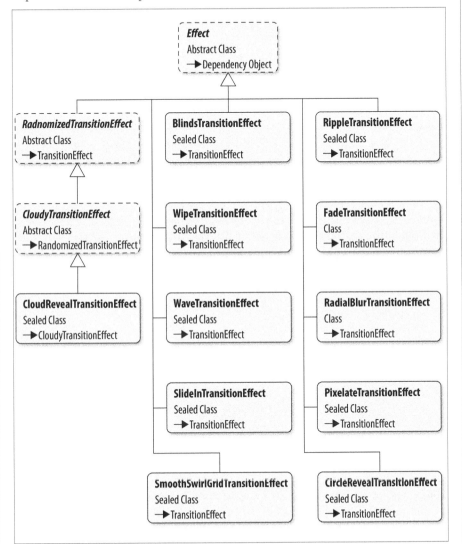

Figure 5-23. Transition effect diagram

We can see what is unique about these effects by looking at their common base class shown in Figure 5-24.

Figure 5-24. TransitionEffect base class

The base class has three properties to examine. For starters, there are the two input properties, `Input` (which contains the destination brush) and `OldImage` (which holds the original image brush). The Progress property indicates the current transition point between the two brushes. A zero value means you see the `OldImage` brush, whereas setting Progress to one or greater means you see the Input brush instead. It is easy to see how these effects are used by the VSM. Just before the animation starts, take a snapshot of both states. Assign the current state to the `OldImage` brush and the destination state to the `Input` brush. Last, create an animation that changes the progress property over the expected duration. Nice!

Blend ships with a few VSM effects. You can create your own custom VSM effect by deriving a class from the `TransitionEffect` class.

Summary

Being able to visualize an effect during the design process is invaluable. It's fortunate that Expression Blend and Visual Studio provide this important functionality. Regrettably, neither tool gives you the same rich features when writing custom HLSL code. Once you decide to create your own custom HLSL shader, you might as well use notepad and a command line compiler, as you get no help from either of the Microsoft tools.

Since the premier XAML tools are deficient, creating a shader and its managed .NET wrapper is tiresome and error prone. The lack of automatic tools means that coding, compiling and testing the shader in a XAML application is still a manual process. But don't fret: the next chapter showcases the Shazzam Shader editor tool, an application written years ago to solve this very problem.

CHAPTER 6

Using the Shazzam Shader Editor

Shazzam is a free standalone shader editor that contains all the tools you need to compile, test, and visualize your custom pixel shaders. It automatically generates your managed C# and VB code, provides a rich HLSL editor, and includes all the samples shown in this book.

 You can find the installer for Shazzam at shazzam-tool.com (*http://shaz zam-tool.com*). For more information about installing Shazzam, see the preface in this book.

UI Tour

Let's start with a tour of the Shazzam UI (see Figure 6-1).

The Shazzam interface is comprised of four general areas. On the top left is the Menu Bar. Immediately below the MenuBar is the Toolbar area. It consists of two important panels, the Shader Loader panel and the Settings panel. On the top right side lives the Preview and Samples area. The lower right side contains the Code and Testing tabs. To demonstrate these areas and the rest of the IDE, we'll create and edit a new project in Shazzam.

Create a Custom Shader

We'll start by configuring the default shader file location and then creating a custom shader. If you haven't changed the default configuration, the Shader Loader is open and visible on the left side of the screen. The loader provides an easy way to load existing HLSL files into the editor. As you can see in Figure 6-2, there are three tabs (Your Folder, Sample Shaders, and Tutorial) available in Shader Loader. Click the Change Location link on the Your Folder tab to change location where Shazzam reads and saves *.fx* files.

Figure 6-1. Shazzam UI

Click the File→New Shader File menu or press Ctrl-N to open the new Shader File dialog (Figure 6-3).

The New File dialog opens to the directory configured in the Shader Loader. For this experiment, name your shader file ColorModifier and click Save, then click Yes when asked to create the file. Shazzam creates a text file, populates it with some boilerplate HLSL code, and then loads the file into the editor pane on the lower-right side of the IDE.

 Shazzam defaults to the *.fx* extension for shader files.

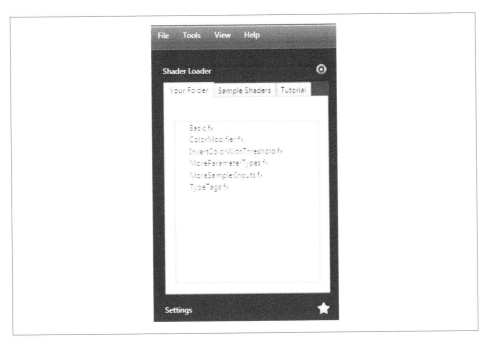

Figure 6-2. Shader Loader, with three tabs

Exploring the HLSL Code Editor

New shaders in Shazzam are populated with a few lines of skeleton code. Example 6-1 shows the code: it's a simplistic pass-through shader that has no effect on the output pixels.

Example 6-1. Boilerplate code in new shader (HLSL)

```
sampler2D input : register(s0);

// new HLSL shader
// modify the comment parameters to reflect your shader parameters

/// <summary>Explain the purpose of this variable.</summary>
/// <minValue>05/minValue>
/// <maxValue>10</maxValue>
/// <defaultValue>3.5</defaultValue>
float SampleInputParam : register(C0);

float4 main(float2 uv : TEXCOORD) : COLOR {

  float4 color;
 color= tex2D( input , uv.xy);

  return color;
}
```

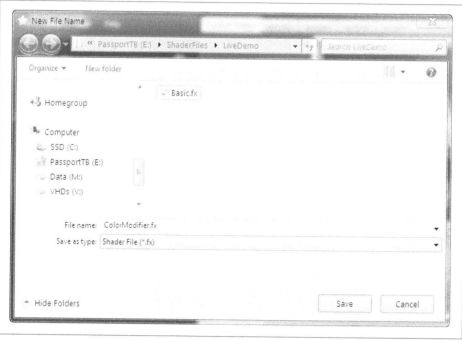

Figure 6-3. New Shader dialog

The editor includes some rudimentary auto-text (Intellisense) as shown in Figure 6-4. As you type new code in the editor, a dropdown list appears containing keyword suggestions. Auto-complete is available for keywords and variable types. Press the spacebar when the desired keyword is selected in the list to have Shazzam insert the code snippet.

A floating context help window is shown whenever the auto-text dropdown is visible.

It's time to change the boilerplate HLSL and create a more interesting shader. Modify the HLSL code in the main function to look like the following example (Example 6-2).

Example 6-2. Modified shader code (HLSL)

```
float4 color;
color= tex2D( input , uv.xy);
float4 invertedColor = float4(color.a - color.rgb, color.a);
return invertedColor;
```

Compiling and Testing the Shader

Developers of all backgrounds are familiar with the compile, debug, and test cycle that dominates programming work. It's such a common cycle that it becomes ingrained into our work habits. UI developers have the additional need to see the UI under

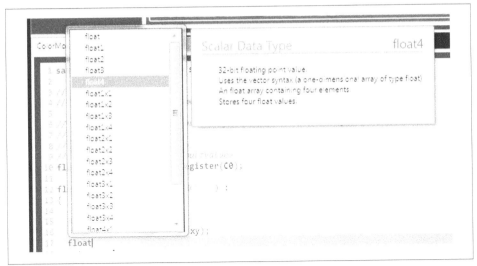

Figure 6-4. Shazzam auto-text and context help

development. Tools like Visual Studio include UI designer tools for these purposes; they let you visualize the UI during the development process.

Shazzam provides similar life cycle tools, giving you the means to compile, test, and visualize your HLSL code. Compiling is easy: press F7 to invoke the built-in compiler.

Since a shader is intended to modify graphical output, you'll want to test it on sample outputs. Across the top-right side of the Shazzam IDE are a number of preview and sample tabs, each containing a sample for assessing your new shader. Table 6-1 shows a list of the included tabs.

Table 6-1. Shazzam preview/sample tabs

Tab Name	Description
Custom Image tabs	Use your own image for the effect preview. The ColorWheel image is provided as default.
Sample1 through Sample4	Colorful sample pictures with suitable color ranges.
ColorWheel	Colorwheel image; represents all 16 million colors in the standard color range.
Squares	Black and white checkerboard pattern, good for testing distortion effects.
Sample UI	Interactive UI, good for testing effects on interface controls.
Media	Short media clip; defaults to auto-play and repeat.
Compare	Compare image with effect and without effect in same window.

 To see the test samples without a shader applied, press F6.

Change the custom image by choosing File→Open Image File (Ctrl-I). I've imported the flower picture seen in the earlier chapters. You can also change the video shown on the Media tab by choosing File→Open Media File (Ctrl-M).

Now, it's time to compile the shader and apply it to the preview images. There are a few compiler tools listed at the top of the Tools menu (see Figure 6-5).

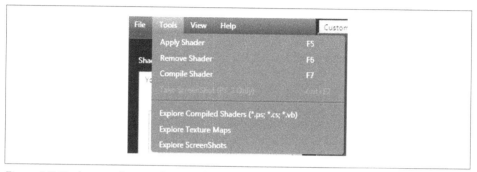

Figure 6-5. Tools menu showing the compiler tools

The tools are self-titled and easy to comprehend. The Compile Shader menu (F7) runs the DirectX compiler on your HLSL code and produces a *.ps* file. Choosing Apply Shader (F5) compiles the shader code and also generates a .NET ShaderEffect class. Then Shazzam applies the finished effect to the samples in the test tabs. To remove the shader, use the Remove Shader menu item (F6).

Here's what my copy of the ColorModifier looks like (Figure 6-6) in the Compare tab.

Figure 6-6. ColorModifier shader shown in the Compare tab

Editor Status Bar

The editor status bar is located at the bottom edge of the code window. It provides three bits of feedback regarding your shader code. During normal operations, it contains a green info-tip that shows the last compile time. When the file has unsaved changes, there is a yellow info-tip explaining this unsaved status. When there is a compile error, a red info-tip appears. Figure 6-7 shows all three info-tips in action.

```
14
15    float4 color;
16    color= texof( input , uv.xy);
17    float4 invertedColor = floa4(color.a - color.rgb, color.a);
18    return invertedColor;
19 |
```

E:\Projects\ShazzamPaid\Shazzam\bin\Release\memory(17,26): error X3004: undeclared identifier 'floa4'   Last Compiled at 6:00:08 PM   Shader not saved.

Figure 6-7. Status bar with three info-tips

The warning info-tip provides vital information when you have a compile error. The error in this example is due to a misspelling of the `float4` keyword on line 17. The into-tip shows the current error description and error location. Double-clicking the warning tip applies an orange highlight to the offending code line, making it easier to find the error.

 Be sure to fix any compiler errors before continuing.

Shazzam also shows the compiler progress during a compile. Press F5 and keep an eye on the status area. There is a short animation bar shown on the green info-tip during compilation.

Exploring the Generated Code

I've drummed home a point many times in this book: to create a custom shader, you need several files. Let's review. You need an HLSL text file, the binary *.ps* file produced by the shader compiler, and a .NET code file (*.cs* or *.vb*) that implements the managed effect class. In Shazzam, you create the HLSL file and it produces the other files.

You can see the contents of the C# file by clicking on the `Generated Shader - C#` tab (see Figure 6-8). If your prefer Visual Basic, there is also a tab containing the VB generated code.

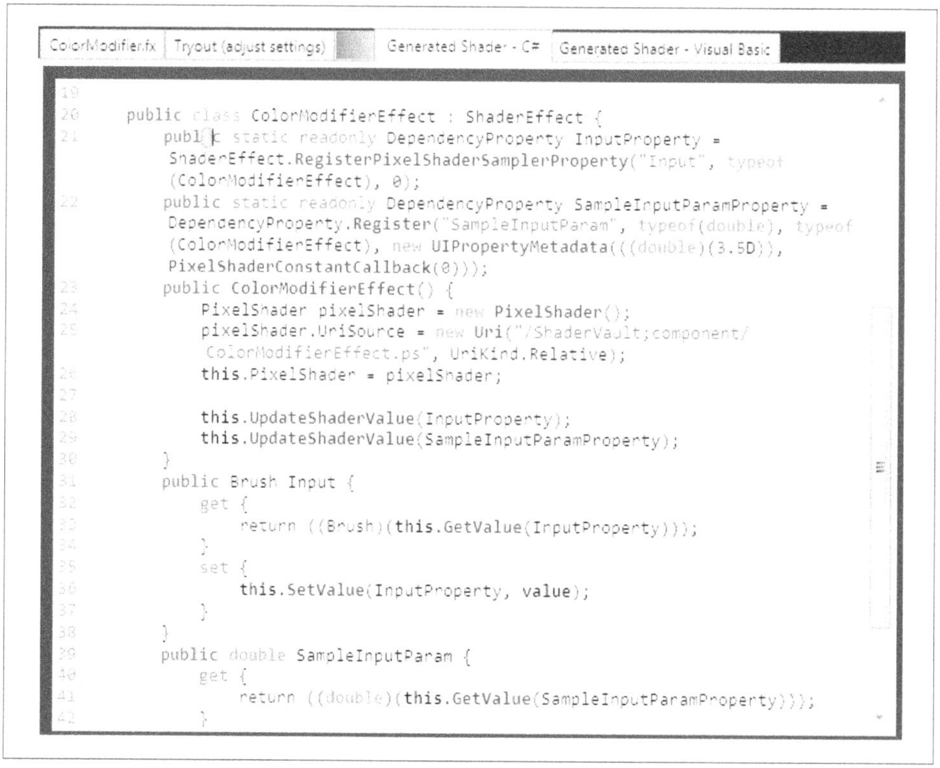

ColorModifier.fx
Tryout (adjust settings)
Generated Shader - C#
Generated Shader - Visual Basic
19
20 public class ColorModifierEffect : ShaderEffect {
21 public static readonly DependencyProperty InputProperty = ShaderEffect.RegisterPixelShaderSamplerProperty("Input", typeof (ColorModifierEffect), 0);
22 public static readonly DependencyProperty SampleInputParamProperty = DependencyProperty.Register("SampleInputParam", typeof(double), typeof (ColorModifierEffect), new UIPropertyMetadata(((double)(3.5D)), PixelShaderConstantCallback(0)));
23 public ColorModifierEffect() {
24 PixelShader pixelShader = new PixelShader();
25 pixelShader.UriSource = new Uri("/ShaderVault;component/ ColorModifierEffect.ps", UriKind.Relative);
26 this.PixelShader = pixelShader;
27
28 this.UpdateShaderValue(InputProperty);
29 this.UpdateShaderValue(SampleInputParamProperty);
30 }
31 public Brush Input {
32 get {
33 return ((Brush)(this.GetValue(InputProperty)));
34 }
35 set {
36 this.SetValue(InputProperty, value);
37 }
38 }
39 public double SampleInputParam {
40 get {
41 return ((double)(this.GetValue(SampleInputParamProperty)));
42 }

Figure 6-8. Generated Shader - C# tab, showing the code

Shazzam creates a dependency property for every sampler input (`S` register) and shader constant (`C` register). Looking at the generated C# code, you can see a generated dependency property for the sampler `Input` (line 21) and another for the `SampleInputParam` parameter (line 22). It also configures matching .NET property wrappers (lines 31 and 39).

Review the HLSL code to determine where these properties are declared. For fun, try changing the HLSL parameter names and recompiling the shader to see what influence renaming has on the generated code.

Changing Options

Shazzam has an option panel for changing the appearance of the IDE and configuring the build options. You can find the Settings panel by clicking on the Settings header on the left side of the IDE. Figure 6-9 show the options available in this panel.

The settings available in this panel are reasonably self-explanatory; here is a brief overview of each setting.

Figure 6-9. Settings Panel

The `Target Framework` option tells the DirectX compiler whether to target the PS2 or PS3 specifications. Choosing Silverlight is the same as targeting WPF PS2 with the added benefit that the generated .NET effect class is optimized for the Silverlight runtime.

The `Generated Namespace` option specifies which namespace is added to the generated C#/VB code. Here is an example of a C# file with the default namespace added.

```
namespace Shazzam.Shaders {

    public class ColorModifierEffect : ShaderEffect {}}
```

Set your indentation preferences for the code editor with the `Indentation` option.

The `Default Animation Length` option specifies the default length of animations available in the testing harness.

Working with HLSL Parameters

A useful .NET effect exposes properties for manipulating the shader input parameters. In this section, we'll add a new input property to the HLSL and experiment with the Shazzam comment tags.

The first step in the process is to modify the code in the main method, as shown here (Example 6-3).

Example 6-3. Modify HLSL so half the image color is inverted (HLSL)

```
float4 color;
color= tex2D( input , uv.xy);
if(uv.x > .5 ){
  float4 invertedColor = float4(color.a - color.rgb, color.a);
  return invertedColor;
}
return color;
```

Figure 6-10 shows the results after the modified code is compiled. One-half of the image is rendered in the original colors; the other half is depicted with inverted colors.

Figure 6-10. Half Inverted Image

Let's make the divide location customizable. Add a new input parameter named `Divid ingLine` to the top of the HLSL code.

```
float DividingLine : register(C1) ;
```

Then modify the `if` statement to use the new parameter, as shown in Example 6-4.

Example 6-4. Use the DividingLine parameter (HLSL)

```
float4 color;
color= tex2D( input , uv.xy);
if(uv.x > DividingLine ){
  float4 invertedColor = float4(color.a - color.rgb, color.a);
return invertedColor;
}

return color;
```

Compile and apply the shader, then check out the results. Because the default value for a float parameter is zero, the dividing line is no longer visible. To see the dividing line, we'll use the testing portion of the Shazzam IDE.

Testing Parameters

Shazzam creates a test harness for every input parameter. Click on the `Tryout` (`adjust settings`) tab to see the auto-generated testers. Figure 6-11 shows the two auto-generated test controls for our newly compiled shader. The first tester manipulates the input values for the `SampleInputParam` parameter. The second tester is for our new `DividingLine` parameter.

 SampleInputParam is a parameter included in the boilerplate HLSL code.

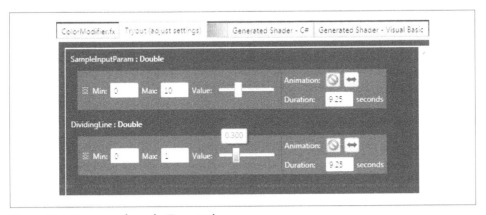

Figure 6-11. Test controls on the Tryout tab

Shazzam examines the data type for each dependency property to determine what type of test UI to create. Since the `DividingLine` parameter is a `Double`, you get a single slider control to change the parameter value. Drag the `DividingLine` slider to change the parameter value and observe the changes in the rendered output; the dividing line moves horizontally across the screen.

I like dragging sliders as much as any person does, but on a complex effect it can get tedious changing multiple parameters. To automate the parameter changes, Shazzam also provides animation controls on the right edge of each tester row. Click the animate button, the one with the two-headed arrow, to start the animation. The animation runs until you click the stop button.

You can change the duration of the animation while the animation is running or stopped.

The animation duration is customizable for each tester row. As you can see in Figure 6-11, I've changed the length to 9.25 seconds for my animations. Set the length at the global level by changing the animation length in the Settings pane. You can also change the value for each tester row by typing a new value in the animation textbox.

Default Values for Parameters

Shazzam makes some assumptions about your input parameters. For example, when a parameter is typed as an HLSL float, Shazzam assumes that the minimum and default values for the test harness are zero and the maximum value is one. What if the testable range should be different—for example, a minimum test value of 120 and a maximum test value of 1000?

The variety of shaders you can create in HLSL is endless. Shazzam seeds the tester with default values, but the numbers assigned are an arbitrary choice. Without your help, Shazzam doesn't really know what test values are significant to your shader inputs.

Changing the test harness values

One solution is to edit the range values in the tester control. Type the desired value in the min and max textboxes, as shown in Figure 6-12. Shazzam automatically updates the slider control to the new range values.

When you recompile the shader, the test controls are reset to the default values (minimum = 0, maximum = 1). That can be annoying, as you need to reconfigure the test control each time you return to the Tryout tab. To mitigate that pain, you can use Shazzam XML tags to influence the tester defaults.

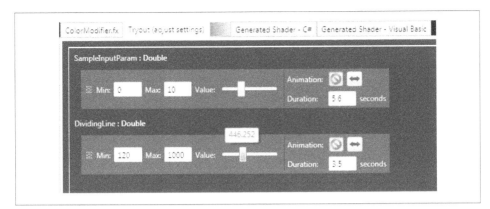

Figure 6-12. Change min and max range values

Shazzam Tags

Use the Shazzam XML tags to convey information to the compiler and test harness. If you have used the C# XML comments in your managed code, the syntax will be familiar. Add a Shazzam tag to the HLSL code with the triple slash syntax (Example 6-5).

Example 6-5. Shazzam XML tag syntax

```
/// <summary>Summary info here...</summary>
float2 MyPoint1: register(C0);
```

By embedding them in a comment, they are ignored by the DirectX compiler. Let's look at an example to see how they are used.

In Figure 6-13, I've set the minimum test value to .25, the maximum test value to .75, and the default value to 0.3. I'm also using the <summary> tag. This causes Shazzam to add an XML comment to the ShaderEffect's dependency property.

```
12 /// <summary>The horizontal location for the dividing line.  0=left, 1=right</summary>
13 /// <minValue>0.25</minValue>
14 /// <maxValue>.75</maxValue>
15 /// <defaultValue>.3</defaultValue>
16 float DividingLine : register(C1) ;
```

Figure 6-13. Shazzam tags in HLSL editor

Compile the shader and check out the Tryout tab (Figure 6-14). Notice how the textbox and slider controls match the Shazzam tag values. Shazzam also generates a tooltip showing the summary information.

Tables 6-2 and 6-3 show a list of available tags and a short description of how they influence the Shazzam compiler and test harness.

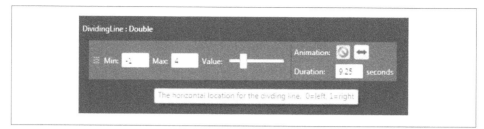

Figure 6-14. Tester, showing new defaults and tooltip

Table 6-2. Shazzam tags, general and class level

Shazzam Tag	Description
///	A Shazzam XML comment tag. Content is ignored by the DirectX compiler.
<class>	Specifies the desired classname for generated file. By default, Shazzam uses the filename for the effect name. A class named SwirlyEffect is generated from the Swirly.fx file. Use the <class> tag to override the default name.
<namespace>	Specifies the desired namespace for the effect class. By default, Shazzam uses the namespace configured in the Tools panel settings panel. Use the <namespace> tag to override the default namespace name.
<description>	Provides a description for this effect. Shazzam will generate comments in the .cs/.vb file from this description.
<target>	Forces the compiler to generate a Silverlight or WPF version of the .NET effect class. The default target is configured in the Settings panel. Use the <target> tag to override the default target.
<type>	Use the <type> tag to change the default .NET type specified for the generated dependency property.

Table 6-3. Shazzam Tags, parameter level

Shazzam Tag	Description
<summary>	This tag is used by the Tryout tab.
	It is used on a shader input parameter to describe the purpose of the input parameter. It causes a tooltip to show in Shazzam for the test control.
<minValue>	This tag is used by the Tryout tab.
	It provides an initial value for the minimum textbox.
<maxValue>	This tag is used by the Tryout tab.
	It provides an initial value for the maximum textbox.
<defaultValue>	This tag is used by the Tryout tab.
	It provides a starting value for the value slider.

Input Parameter Types

The examples I have presented in this chapter so far have used the float data type.

In addition to the float data type, HLSL offers a limited set of other types for shader parameters. The following HLSL (Figure 6-15) demonstrates parameters declared with the float2 and float4 data types.

```
3
4 /// <summary>Float2 contains 2 float values. Maps to Point or Size in .NET.</summary>
5 float2 MyTwoValues : register(C0);
6 /// <summary>Float4 contains 4 float values. Maps to Color or Point4D in .NET.</summary>
7 float4 MyColor: register(C0);
8
```

Figure 6-15. float2 and float4 parameter types

The float2 type is registered as the Point type on the .NET side, while float4 produces a dependency property of type Color. The Shazzam testing harness detects the new parameter types and fabricates a different testing UI (see Figure 6-16).

For the Point value, Shazzam creates a tester with two sliders. For the Color value, it provides a visual color picker control. The animation controls change a bit, too. For the Color value, you select a beginning and ending color and the animation smoothly transitions between the two. For the Point animation, you have two choices. The first animation button (with the diagonal arrows) starts an animation that moves from the upper-left to lower-right corners of the preview tab. The second animation button (with the circular arrows) triggers a circular animation, which moves the point around the outside edge of the preview tab.

Influencing the .NET Type

Shazzam chooses the type for the generated dependency property based on the HLSL type. For example, a property of type float2 is translated to a .NET Point type. Example 6-6 shows how to use the <type> tag to override the default code generation behavior.

Example 6-6. Use the Shazzam <type> tag (HLSL)

```
/// <summary>Default mapping  of HLSL float2 is to .NET Point</summary>
float2 MyPoint1: register(C0);

/// <type>Point</type>
/// <summary>Use specific mapping to Point</summary>
float2 MyPoint2: register(C1);

/// <type>Size</type>
/// <summary>Use specific mapping to Size</summary>
float2 MySize: register(C2);
```

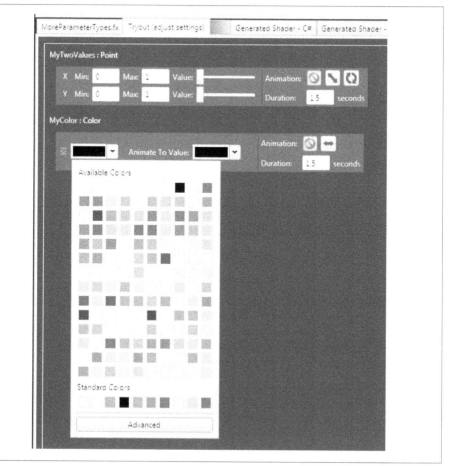

Figure 6-16. Tester controls with Point and Color editors

```
/// <type>Vector</type>
/// <summary>Use specific mapping to Vector</summary>
float2 MyVector: register(C3);
```

The code snippet in Example 6-7 shows the resulting C# dependency properties generated by Shazzam. Take note of the .NET types and see how they match the <type> tag used in the previous HLSL example.

Example 6-7. Generated C# dependency properties

```
public static readonly DependencyProperty MyPoint1Property =
  DependencyProperty.Register("MyPoint1",
  typeof(Point), typeof(TypeTagsEffect),
  new UIPropertyMetadata(new Point(OD, OD),
  PixelShaderConstantCallback(0)));

public static readonly DependencyProperty MyPoint2Property =
```

```
DependencyProperty.Register("MyPoint2",
  typeof(Point), typeof(TypeTagsEffect),
  new UIPropertyMetadata(new Point(OD, OD),
  PixelShaderConstantCallback(1)));

public static readonly DependencyProperty MySizeProperty =
  DependencyProperty.Register("MySize",
  typeof(Size), typeof(TypeTagsEffect),
  new UIPropertyMetadata(new Size(OD, OD)\
  PixelShaderConstantCallback(2)));

public static readonly DependencyProperty MyVectorProperty =
  DependencyProperty.Register("MyVector",
  typeof(Vector), typeof(TypeTagsEffect),
  new UIPropertyMetadata(new Vector(OD, OD),
  PixelShaderConstantCallback(3)));
```

The HLSL to .NET type mappings are shown in Table 6-4.

Table 6-4. Type tag mappings, with defaults

HLSL type	Default .NET type	Alternate .NET types
float	Double	Single
float2	Point	Size, Vector
float3	Point3D	Vector3D[a]
float4	Color	Point4D[a]

[a] Available in WPF, but not in Silverlight

Multi-Input Shaders

Psst, I'll let you in a little secret. If you want to have some real fun with shaders, expand the number of input textures. Once you have a few input textures, you can combine the pixels in amazing ways.

Use the `Sample2D` syntax to declare multiple sample inputs in the HLSL code (Example 6-8).

Example 6-8. Declare three input samplers (HLSL)

```
sampler2D inputA : register(s0);
sampler2D inputB : register(s1);
sampler2D inputC : register(s2);
```

Example 6-9 shows how to work with two of the shader inputs. The code combines the colors from `inputA` and `inputB` into the final output. Note how the code examines the red channel of the second texture to determine whether to make the combined pixel a grayscale value.

Example 6-9. Multi-input shader code (HLSL)

```
/// <defaultValue>.4</defaultValue>
float RedThreshold : register(C0);

float4 main(float2 uv : TEXCOORD) : COLOR {

  float4 color1= tex2D( inputA , uv.xy);
  float4 color2= tex2D( inputB , uv.xy);
  if(color2.r > RedThreshold ){
    color1.rgb = lerp(color2.r, color1.b,.9);
  }

  return color1;
}
```

Where does Shazzam get the input pixels for each of the shader inputs? The sampler data for the first parameter (the one in the s0 register) comes from the sample images provided on each preview tab. To change the image for the other sampler input parameters (s1 and s2 registers) use the Tryout tab.

When Shazzam encounters a Sampler2D input, it generates an image picker control in the tester UI. As you can see in Figure 6-17, there is one image picker on the test page for each additional input parameter.

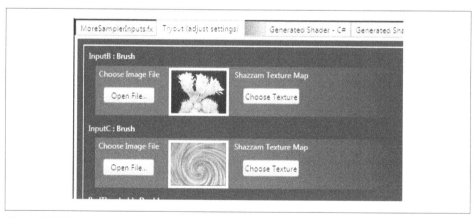

Figure 6-17. Two image pickers

Shazzam includes over 20 built-in textures. Access them by clicking the Choose Texture button and choosing from the floating list (see Figure 6-18). If none of the included images suit your fancy, click on the Open File... button to choose your own image.

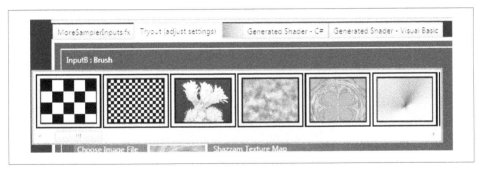

Figure 6-18. Texture chooser

I picked the big checkerboard texture for my `InputB` image. This is what the combined image looks like in the Shazzam IDE (Figure 6-19).

Figure 6-19. Combine two samplers into grayscale

Shader Loader

Shazzam ships with a ton of sample HLSL files. You can use the File→Open Shader File menu to open other files or use the Shader Loader panel for instant access to the included library. The loader has three sections, each providing access to a different set of shader files.

Your Folder tab

This is where you'll find your custom shaders. Click on the `Change Location` link to explore any folder on your computer. Shazzam shows that folder as the default view, and lets you drill down into the subfolders (Figure 6-20).

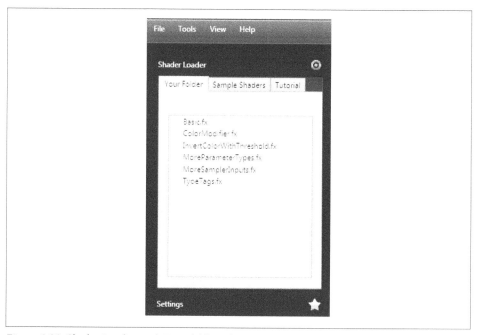

Figure 6-20. Shader Loader, with Your folder tab open

Sample Shaders tab

The `Sample Shaders` section of the `Shader Loader` contains dozens of example shaders. The code in these samples comes from many sources. Some of the samples are from the Microsoft shader project published on Codeplex. Others come from the XAML community or from my late-night, caffeine-induced shader experiments.

 The XAML community is a charitable group of people. My inbox often contains emails from Shazzam users who are excited to share their latest HLSL nuggets. I'd enjoy reading about your shader explorations too, so send a copy of your latest invention to *shazzam@scandiasoft.com* when you are done.

The Tutorial tab

In this section, you'll find a set of categorized and commented tutorial shaders. The ideas and examples in this section were first created to fill the documentation void for

XAML/Shader developers. Working on new content for this section eventually led to the creation of the book you are reading. The pathway goes in both directions; many of the examples in this book have been added to the tutorial section in Shazzam.

More Shazzam Tools

We've seen most of the Shazzam IDE at this point. There are a few more tools to investigate before closing the chapter.

Fullscreen mode

Show the image previews in full-screen mode by choosing the View→Full Screen Image menu (F9). This hides the toolbar and code windows. Use the Escape or F9 key to toggle back to split-screen mode.

Show the code window in full-screen mode by choosing the View→Full Screen Code menu (F10). This hides the toolbar and image preview windows. Use the Escape or F10 key to toggle back to split screen mode.

Take a screenshot

I love writing shaders and experimenting with the shader properties on the Tryout tab. Before long, I'll have a bunch of test animations running and find myself mesmerized by the artistic images playing on the screen. You can capture the active shader with the screenshot tool by pressing Ctrl-F2 at any time in Shazzam, even while test animations are running.

Due to a limitation in the WPF API, you cannot capture a screenshot if you are targeting the PS_3 specification. In addition, you are limited to capturing the effect applied to the image in the Custom Image tab. None of the other sample images or UI are capturable.

The screenshots are stored in a folder under the Shazzam install location. Just use the Tools→Explore Screenshots menu to peruse your screenshot masterpieces.

Copying the Files into a Visual Studio Project

To use your shader in a Visual Studio or Expression Blend project requires importing a *.ps* and *.cs* file. Shazzam generates these files during the compile process and places them in a dedicated folder. You can find the physical files by choosing the Tools→Explore Compiled Shaders menu item (see Figure 6-5). Shazzam creates a folder for each compiled effect. On my computer, the generated files for my *ColorModifier.fx* shader are inside the ColorModifierEffect directory.

Summary

Shazzam makes quick work of the shader creation and testing process. Be sure and check out the Sample Shaders and Tutorial sections available in the Shader Loader. There are more than one hundred shaders tucked away in there, enough to keep an effects junkie happy for a long time.

We've traveled a long road to get to this point in the book. By now, you should be comfortable with shaders and understand the nuances of the effects API in the .NET framework. You've seen the effects tools in Visual Studio, Blend, and Shazzam. It's finally time to dig deeper into the details of the HLSL programming language.

CHAPTER 7

HLSL in Detail

HLSL is a part of the C family of programming languages. Many familiar C icons/ constructs are part of its specifications, such as creating blocks of code with curly brackets, requiring case-sensitive tokens, and using a semicolon to terminate a code statement. It sports a pocket-sized API containing a few hundred keywords and contains several dozen helpful shader functions.

 HLSL is a moniker for the High Level Shader Language.

HLSL, at its core, is a language optimized for creating small, specialized programs, which manipulate the graphics pipeline data on the GPU. Through HLSL, we have the power to control important graphical constructs like vertex and pixel shaders. To harness this power requires learning a new programming language and API. Just as importantly, you need to change your brain—remap your neurons to a different way of thinking about graphics code.

Parallel Processing in Shaders

.NET programmers are often delighted to find that shaders are nothing more than a miniature program that is optimized to run on the computer's GPU. This happiness fades when they start exploring the strange programming model underlying shaders, however. Because shaders run on massive parallel processors, developers shouldn't use their traditional OO or procedural approach to writing shader code.

Raise your hand if you've ever written pixel manipulation code that walks though the X and Y coordinates of the underlying image. I see a few *GDI* developers sheepishly waving their hands in the air. In GDI, that was an accepted practice. You'd loop through the pixel array and call the `GetPixel` and `SetPixel` functions to manipulate the pixels. Using nested `for` loops to manipulate pixels in this fashion is time-consuming, however.

It's like swimming across a pool of molasses—not recommended if you are concerned about performance.

On the .NET Framework side, there are a few classes for speedy pixel manipulation. I'm referring to the `MemoryMappedFile` and `WriteableBitmap` classes. While these classes are major improvements over their GDI brethren, their performance is dwarfed by the sheer power of shader code running on a GPU.

Parallelism and the GPU

GPUs are inherently parallel in nature and are designed to run concurrent operations. Essentially, they are packed with hundreds of data-parallel, floating-point processors. To take advantage of data parallelism, you create code that works with a small isolated portion of a data structure. If done right, the data modification algorithm can solve the problem while running simultaneously on many processors.

Another term favored by the industry for a GPU processor is "shader unit".

The data structure for a pixel shader is the image data and the data modification algorithm is the custom shader code. Your pixel shader function is run once for each pixel location, with many instances of the code running simultaneously on the GPU.

Your HLSL code is responsible for outputting a color value for ONE pixel. In order to process all the pixels on a 1920 × 1080 monitor, the GPU runs the shader algorithm more than two million times, once for each pixel. Currently there are no consumer-level GPUs that can handle two million transactions in one pass, so the job is divided into many sub-batches. The more powerful the GPU, the fewer batches needed.

One-Pixel-at-a-Time Algorithm

Parallel processing requires a different mindset from traditional single-path development. Thinking in terms of columns and rows, dividing an image into a checkerboard of tiny squares is wrong headed. You need to modernize your brain and embrace the notion of the single pixel algorithm.

Try this thought experiment. Write a shader that sets every pixel in the third row (y==3) to an orange color. Are you thinking about setting the y value to three and moving horizontally across the row of pixels changing the color as you go?

Bzzzt. You lose.

Remember, you're working in mono pixel land. The shader code runs once for each pixel with the framework providing the location of the current pixel (Example 7-1).

Example 7-1. Main shader function, with location parameter

```
// the currentLocation parameter indicates the
// location of the pixel being processed
float4 main(float2 currentLocation : TEXCOORD) : COLOR
{

    // code that changes the current pixel color
    //...
}
```

In this realm, there are no rows, just a single solitary pixel. Every decision made in the shader relates to this single pixel; it's the major point of reference for your code.

The Relationship Between DirectX and the GPU

Output displays come in many sizes and shapes. A modern phone display packs a dense set of pixels into a tiny handheld screen. Regardless of the size of the display, most modern monitors expect their input in a certain format, known as a *frame buffer*.

A GPU is a specialized chipset that generates frame buffers for the display monitor. Inside the GPU is a wealth of graphics production tools and other specialized algorithms. It contains sophisticated rendering engines, plus a collection of transformation, clipping, masking, and other graphics tools. Working directly with the GPU is not a job for the faint-hearted. Instead, you should choose a rendering API that knows how to work with the low-level GPU features.

In the Windows world, the two dominant rendering API's are DirectX and OpenGL. Microsoft DirectX is a family of multimedia libraries distributed within a single SDK. Nested within the DirectX SDK is a diverse collection of graphics tools. The two we are interested in for this chapter are the Direct3D API and it companion HLSL programming language.

Understanding Registers

Pixel shaders rely on GPU registers, using them to read and store data. GPU registers are special high-speed storage areas within the hardware. Direct3D provides access to the registers, subdividing them into categories.

To access information in a register, create an input variable with the register keyword. This is done at the top of the shader program and looks similar to a global variable declaration.

```
float a2 : register(C0);
```

In HLSL, each register category is identified by a prefix specified in the register syntax (C, S, T, etc.—see Example 7-2).

Example 7-2. Register prefixes

```
// Useful in XAML effects
sampler2D a1 : register(S0); // Sampler register
float     a2 : register(C0); // Constant float register

// less common registers
float4    a3 : register(T0); // Texture register
int       a4 : register(I0); // Constant Integer register
bool      a5 : register(B0); // Constant Boolean register


// framework registers (unlikely to use these)
float     a6 : register(V0); // Input Color register
float     a7 : register(R0); // Temporary register
float     a8 : register(P0); // Predicate register
```

The **Sampler** and **Constant Float** registers are indispensable for writing effective shaders. You'll learn more about registers later in this chapter.

Basic Structure of an HLSL Program

All pixel shaders require a starting function. By convention, that function is named `main` or `Main` but the entry function name can be any non-reserved word. When you compile the code with the DirectX compiler (*fxc.exe*), you specify the starting function name. Shazzam assumes your entry function is named `main`.

 In HLSL, the term **function** is customary when referring to a named section of code, rather than the .NET term **method**.

Shaders have an input declaration area. Place all shader level declares at the top of the code file. Items declared at this level are available within all shader functions (Example 7-3).

Example 7-3. Shader declarations

```
// use top of text file to declare
// shader level inputs and constants
sampler2D input : register(s0);

// declare the entry function
float4 main(float2 uv : TEXCOORD) : COLOR
{
  return GetBlackColor();
}
```

User-Defined Functions

User-defined functions consist of a declaration line, a pair of curly brackets, and a zero or more code statements (Example 7-4).

Example 7-4. User-defined function prototype

```
[prefix] returntype functionName (parameters)
{ statements;}
```

The function prefix is not a scoping keyword, like **public** or **private**; it's a compiler instruction (static, inline, target). For example, the following asks the compiler to inline the function inside the calling function.

```
inline void function1(){}
```

Decades of coding experience teach that it's best to break code into well named, loosely coupled functions. A shader can contain many functions, one of which is designated the main function. The one restriction on using additional functions is that they must be declared in the text file above the calling function. Code order matters (Example 7-5).

Example 7-5. Declaring and using another function

```
sampler2D input : register(s0);

inline float4 GetBlackColor(){
  return float4(0,0,0,1);
}
float4 main(float2 uv : TEXCOORD) : COLOR
{
  return GetBlackColor();
}
```

Function parameters are defined in a parameter list and can have the following parameter prefixes (as seen in Table 7-1).

Table 7-1. Function parameter prefixes

Prefix	Description
in	This is the default behavior. A parameter without a prefix is considered an in parameter.
	The value is passed into the function but changes to parameter do not affect value in caller.
out	Indicates that the value is considered an out/result value. A change to this parameter affects the value in the caller.
inout	Indicates the value is considered both in and out.
uniform	Same as the in prefix, but signifies the data is a constant value.

Functions that have a non-void return type must have at least one line of code that returns a value of the correct type.

Due to hardware limitations, recursive functions are forbidden.

Semantics

One of the major benefits of the DirectX model is that is uses a flexible, pipeline approach to rendering the graphical output (Figure 7-1).

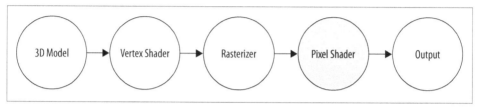

Figure 7-1. DirectX Pipeline

Each shader receives input, does some computation work, and passes the modified information further down the pipeline chain. Semantics are a form of metadata attached to variables and other parts of your shader code. As data is passed through the HLSL pipeline, DirectX uses the semantic information to determine how to treat parameters. These are not something you can ignore; semantics are required for variables passed between shader stages.

In the standard DirectX world, the input from the pixel shader comes from the vertex shader. Let's look at how the semantics are used in the vertex shader.

 Vertex shaders are not discussed in detail in this book because they are not available to WPF programs or standard Silverlight applications. Silverlight applications that partake of the XNA integration are the exception to this rule.

Imagine you are writing a vertex shader and want to pass a group of values to your pixel shader. You define the following **struct** (Example 7-6).

Example 7-6. HLSL struct definition

```
struct OutputStruct {
    float4 Position;
    float4 Color;
    float4 OtherPoints;
    float2 TextureSampleLocation;
};
```

At the end of your vertex shader code, you'd populate the **struct** and return it from the function call. DirectX takes the **struct** data and stores it in certain registers, rasterizes the vertex information, and passes the `struct` data to the next shader stage. The problem, as the DirectX engine sees it, is that it doesn't know which of the `float4` members is the color value and which is the position value. To mitigate this problem, HLSL uses semantics, a simple bit of metadata attached to data or function parameters. All variables passed between shader stages must have semantic keywords applied.

The syntax is straightforward (see Example 7-7); declare the parameter, type a colon, and use the semantic keyword.

Example 7-7. HLSL struct with semantic keywords

```
struct OutputStruct {
    float4 Position : ;
    float4 Color : COLOR;
    float4 OtherPoints;
    float2 TextureSampleLocation : TEXCOORD;
};
```

The output from the vertex shader becomes an input for the pixel shader. How do semantic keywords work within this portion of the pipeline? To answer that question, examine the function in Example 7-8.

Example 7-8. Main function with semantic keywords

```
float4 main(float2 uv : TEXCOORD) : COLOR
{
  return float4 (0,0,0,0);
}
```

This `main` function looks familiar; it's the entry point for our shader. Note the two semantic keywords used here (`TEXCOORD, COLOR`) are the same as the ones used in the vertex output. It's a requirement that the main function code use the semantic `TEXCOORD`, for the input parameter. This binds the incoming texture coordinates to our uv variable. Also, our return value (the `float4`) must use the `COLOR` semantic. The compiler refuses to compile entry functions without these semantics.

 A sophisticated pixel shader might return multiple color outputs in a struct. HLSL provides the COLOR0, COLOR1, COLOR2, etc., keywords to map additional float4 values to the COLOR semantic. For our purposes, COLOR and COLOR0 are identical.

There are a couple more semantic keywords available for pixel shaders (`VPOS`, `VFACE`, `DEPTH`) but it's rare to use them in shaders destined for the XAML ecosystem.

Data Types

Data types are a key part of any programming language. In a strongly typed language, you work with a variety of data types, each optimized for storing certain value types. HLSL provides a set of predefined data types, and offers the ability to create custom types.

Shaders run on 3D graphics cards. Modern GPU cards are designed to work efficiently with floating-point numbers. That means that the most cost-effective data-type in HLSL is a float. GPU's are also optimized to work with groups of values (known as vectors). It's actually faster to apply an operation to a vector containing four floats than it is to apply the operation to each float separately.

Scalar type

I've seen a number of half-baked definitions of the word scalar over the years. Here's my take on the word. A scalar variable is destined to hold a single, atomic value, while a composite variable is able to hold multiple values. In HLSL, you declare a scalar variable in the conventional C language fashion (Example 7-9).

Example 7-9. Declare scalar variables

```
float a ; // 32-bit floating point number
int   x ; // 32-bit signed integer
bool  b ; // bool, true or false
half  y ; // 16-bit floating point number
```

HLSL supports a number of data types for variables. It's best to stick with the float type in most scenarios, as not all hardware or PS specifications support non-float types.

Array type

Grouping data values is a popular programming task. The array has existed in the programming world since the early days, the mathematical concept transitioning easily to the binary world of computer data. It's a venerable mechanism for storing many pieces of data in a single variable (Example 7-10).

Example 7-10. Using an array in HLSL

```
float numbers[6];
numbers[0] = 0.2;
numbers[1] = 0.4;
numbers[2] = 0.8;
// ...
float result = numbers[0];

return float4(numbers[0], numbers[1], numbers[2], 1);
```

Vector type

The array maybe familiar but the `vector` and `matrix` types are more common in shader code. To be a shader virtuoso, you need to know these types and their special syntax.

A vector is nothing more than a one-dimensional array. By default, it contains four float values. Because the 3D hardware processes vector operations at supersonic speed, it makes sense that HLSL elevates vectors to first class status.

On the hardware, a vector stores four items. The compiler knows this, and attempts to optimize the code shown in Example 7-11, possibly placing the `dataC` and `dataD` floats in a single hardware vector.

Example 7-11. Declaring vector variables

```
// size value must between 1 and 4
// vector<datatype, size> varName;

vector dataA;           // 4 floats
vector<float, 4> dataB;  // 4 floats

vector<float, 2> dataC;  // 2 floats
vector<float, 2> dataD;  // 2 floats
```

There is an additional syntax for declaring vectors, which is simpler and more common than using the `vector` keyword. It looks odd, if you come from C# or Java background, but it's the standard way to declare vectors (Example 7-12).

Example 7-12. Declare vector with simpler syntax

```
// use the alternate vector syntax

float4 dataE;  // vector with 4 floats
int4   dataF;  // vector with 4 ints
float3 dataG;  // vector with 3 floats
float2 dataH;  // vector with 2 floats
```

Since the vector is just a one-dimensional array, you can access the individual vector items by index, as shown in Example 7-13.

Example 7-13. Accessing individual vector items

```
float result;
float4 myColors;

// access the items in myColors by index
result = myColors[0];
result = myColors[1]; // and myColors[2] and myColors[3]

// access the items in myColors by color indicator
result = myColors.r;
result = myColors.b; // and myColors.g and myColors.a

// access the items in myColors by component indicator
```

```
result = myColors.x;
result = myColors.y; // and myColors.z and myColors.w
```

You can get the vector item using special vector syntax available through the structure (dot) operator. Each position in the array is given a special access letter (`vector.r`, `vector.g`, `vector.b`, `vector.a`, `vector.x`, `vector.y`, `vector.z`, `vector.w`).

Example 7-13 shows how to use the special access letters to refer to an array element.

 These special letters are known as components or component name-spaces. There are two standard component name-spaces, the {x, y, z, w} name-space and the {r, b, g, a} name-space. Either namespace will grant access to the individual vector components. For the sake of read-ability, I suggest using the RGBA namespace when working with a vector that represents a color, but that is not a requirement.

Initializing a vector. Vectors and arrays can be initialized at the time of declaration.

Check out these examples of how to initialize a `float4` variable (Example 7-14).

Example 7-14. Initialize vector variables

```
float4 primaryColor = float4(.2, .4, .6, .8) ; // use the "constructor" syntax
float4 secondaryColor = {.2, .4, .6, .8} ;     // use the "array" syntax
```

This illustrates setting the red channel to .2, the green channel to .4, the blue channel to .6 and the alpha channel to .8.

Swizzling. Once you have defined a vector, you access an individual item with array syntax or component namespace letters, as shown in the previous section. To perform the same operation on multiple items in the vector, there are several routes to take.

Let's say you want to modify three of the four items in the vector. In traditional array syntax, Example 7-15 shows the code that you'd undoubtedly write.

Example 7-15. Traditional way to set three array items to same value

```
float result;
float4 myColors;

myColors[0] = .2 ;
myColors[1] = .2 ;
myColors[2] = .2 ;
```

Another approach to setting multiple array items involves the component namespace syntax (Example 7-16).

Example 7-16. Set three array items to the same value with component syntax

```
// use the special . syntax
myColors.r = myColors.b = myColors.g = .3;
```

I've been looking forward to writing this section on the swizzle syntax since I signed the book contract. The name is evocative and fun to say. In addition, the concept is cool and useful.

Swizzling lets you access the vector items through a combined dot syntax. For example, `vector.rb`, `vector.rbg`, and `vector.argb` are some of the valid combinations permitted in the swizzle syntax.

I'll start by showing you some swizzling examples (Example 7-17) that assign values to the vector items.

Example 7-17. Assign value to vector items via swizzling

```
myColors.bg = .60; // assign value to the blue and green channels
myColors.gb = .65; // order is not important, this is same as previous line
myColors.bb = .70; // not allowed, cannot assign to the same channel more than once

myColors.yz = .75; // using the {x, y, z, w} name-space to assign same channels
myColors.bx = .80; // not allowed, mixing the two name-spaces

myColors.rgb =  .85; // assign three values
myColors.rgba = .90; // assign four values
```

You can use the swizzle to set two, three, or four values in a single assignment. Note that you cannot combine the {x, y, z, w} name-space with the {r, b, g, a} name-space in the same swizzle.

For the next example (7-18), let's create some new vector variables and assign values from an existing vector using the swizzle syntax.

Example 7-18. Assign vector item to vector item

```
float4 myColor = float4(.2, .4, .6, .8) ;
float4 f4 = myColor.bbbb ; // assign the blue value to f4.rgba
f4 =        myColor.b ;    // same as previous line

float2 f2 = myColor.bg ;   // take two of the values and assign to a float2 vector
float3 f3 = myColor.aab ;  // assignments: r=a, b=a, g=b;
f4 =        myColor.ggrr ; // assignments: r=g, b=g, b=r, a=r;
```

Matrix type

The Matrix type is the preferred way to create two-dimensional arrays in HLSL. It's common in HLSL matrix terminology to refer to the array dimension as rows and columns. Matrices are analogous to vectors in many ways. They default to groups of four floats and the compiler will pack matrices for efficiency on the hardware. Example 7-19 shows the syntax for declaring matrices.

Example 7-19. Declaring matrices

```
// create a two dimensional array,
// four floats in 1st dimension, 4 floats in 2nd dimension
// HLSL terminology, four floats in each row, four floats in each column
matrix dataA ;

// create a matrix
// with two rows, three columns
matrix<float, 2, 3> myDataB;

// use the simple matrix declare
float4x4 myDataC ; // four rows, four columns
float3x2 myDataD ; // three rows, two columns
// initialize with values
float3x2 myDataE = { 0.0, 0.1, 0.2, // row 1
                     0.5, 0.6, 0.7 // row 2
                   };
```

Matrices use a component namespace for convenient value access. If you prefer to start the row numbers with zero, use the zero namespace syntax (Table 7-2). For those that favor one-based notation, choose the one-based namespace syntax (Table 7-3).

Table 7-2. Zero-based component namespace

_m00	_m01	_m02	_m03
_m10	_m11	_m12	_m13
_m20	_m21	_m22	_m23
_m30	_m31	_m32	_m33

Table 7-3. One-based component namespace

_11	_12	_13	_14
_21	_22	_23	_24
_32	_32	_33	_34
_41	_42	_43	_44

Here's an example to show the component namespace syntax (Example 7-20).

Example 7-20. Use component namespace in code

```
// use component namespace to assign values
// assign value to row 1, column 1
myDataC._11 = .5;

// assign to same row and column as previous example
//  use the zero based syntax instead
myDataC._m00 = .5;
```

Moreover, matrices have their own swizzle syntax (Example 7-21).

Example 7-21. Matrix swizzle

```
float4x4 myDataC;
myDataC._11_24_33_44 = .9;

float2x2 myDataF = myDataC._44_44_22_22 ;
```

Object type

There are a handful of object types in HLSL. They are primarily used for special composite types and as pointers to intrinsic pipeline items. The ones that are important for XAML effects are listed below. I will disregard the other object types, like string, as they serve no real purpose for the XAML versions of shaders.

Samplers and *Textures* are the two major object types. Newbie HLSL programmers often struggle to comprehend the difference between these two types. Details about these two types appear later in this chapter.

Structures are discussed in the next section; they exist largely to enable programmers to create custom data structures.

Custom type

The main kind of custom type in HLSL is the struct. A struct is a composite type, composed of zero or more members. It consists of field data only, no functions allowed. Be sure and define your custom struct in the HLSL file before it is referenced in the code (Example 7-22).

Example 7-22. Define a custom struct

```
sampler2D input : register(s0);

struct Star
{
  float NumberOfPoints;
  float2 Size;
  float4 FillColor;
  };

float4 main(float2 uv : TEXCOORD) : COLOR
{
  Star s ;
  s.NumberOfPoints = 5;
  s.Size = float2 (1, 1);
  s.FillColor = float4(1, .6, .2, 1);
  // ...
  return float4(1, 1, 1, 1);
}
```

You can also create your own type aliases (a new name for an existing type) with the typedef keyword (Example 7-23).

Example 7-23. Declare a new type alias

```
typedef float3 point3D;

// using the point3D elsewhere
point3D myPoint;
```

Type Casting

Type casting is a fancy name for converting from one type to another. In HLSL, type casting is simple and not fussy. Most of the time, you can just use the assignment operator = and the compiler will cast to the appropriate type. Since floats are the preferred type in shaders, the other scalar types are often converted to floats automatically, especially when the hardware has limitations. Example 7-24 shows the basic syntax for casting one variable to another type.

Example 7-24. Type Casting

```
int count = 4;
float x = 0;
x = count; //  auto cast from int to float
x = (float)count; // use cast operator
```

Some of the basic typecasts that are possible in HLSL are listed in Table 7-4.

Table 7-4. Type Casting Details

Type Conversion	Details
Scalar to Scalar	Always permitted.
int to float	Results in the value being rounded down to nearest whole number.
int to bool, float to bool, bool to int, etc.	Zero is false, Non-zero is true. False is zero, true is 1.
Scalar to Vector	Always permitted. Copies the scalar value to fill a vector location.
Scalar to Matrix	Always permitted. Copies the scalar value to fill a matrix location.
Vector to Vector	Source vector must be same size or smaller than destination.
Matrix to Matrix	Source matrix must be same size or smaller than destination (for both dimensions).
Structure to Scalar, Vector or Matrix	Structure must contain a minimum of one numeric value. For vectors and matrix, the numeric member must be the first member.

There are certain casts that are never permitted: object to vector, object to matrix, and object to scalar types are forbidden as are casts going the opposite direction. It's probably best to show an example of an illegal cast (Example 7-25).

Example 7-25. Illegal cast from Sampler to scalar (float2)

```
sampler s ; // declared at the shader level
------------
```

```
// in main function
float2 z = (float2)s;
// causes a compiler error "Cannot convert from ...."
```

Local Variables

Local variables are declared within a function and are only changeable within the same function. As in any C language, a variable can be declared and initialized on the same line. Variable declarations must include a data type (Example 7-26).

Example 7-26. Local variables

```
float localScope1;       // default value
localScope1 = 3;           // assign value
float localScope2= 100; // initialize value

localScope3 = 80;          // cannot use the variable before the declare
float localScope3;
```

Local variables are truly variable; the value can change during the execution of the function. There are no global variables in HLSL; instead, it has something called *Uniform Input*.

Shader Inputs

Information flows into the shader through different pathways. The DirectX shader pipeline automatically passes information into the shader through function parameters and GPU registers.

TEXCOORD Input

Do you remember the discussion earlier in this chapter about shader semantics? A *semantic* is a special keyword applied to a data type or parameter that informs the pipeline of the items purpose. The current pixel position is passed into your entry function through a parameter marked with the TEXCOORD semantic (Example 7-27).

Example 7-27. Input through the entry function parameter

[C#]

```
// the uv parameter indicates the
// location of the pixel being processed
// the TEXCOORD semantic ensure the the
// pipeline uses the correct float2 value
float4 main(float2 uv : TEXCOORD) : COLOR
```

In the 3D programming world, UV coordinates are 2D coordinates mapped onto a 3D model. Since pixel shaders receive input from the 3D portion of the shader pipeline, the function parameter is usually named *uv*.

The parameter is variable; each time the main function is called, a different pixel location is provided.

Global Variables

Global variables are declared at the top of the shader code module. These items are available in any function within your shader and are also known as Uniform Inputs. While the HLSL specification calls these variables, they act more like read-only fields. Let's look at an example that shows how to declare and initialize a global variable (Example 7-28).

Example 7-28. Declaring global variables

[C#]

```
// implicitly constant/read-only
float globalScope1;      // default value
float globalScope2 = 100; // initialize value

// explicity constant
const float globalScope3 = 200;
```

Once the value is set at the global-level, it cannot be changed in any function body (Example 7-29).

Example 7-29. Illegal assignment to global variable

[C#]

```
  // this assignment is illegal
  globalScope2 = 300;
  // [error X3025: global variables are implicitly constant]
```

Global Inputs

The DirectX pipeline loads information into the GPU registers. To gain access to the GPU registers, you must declare a global input and use the HLSL register keyword, as shown in Example 7-30.

Example 7-30. Declare global input

```
float globalVar = 17 ; // no access to registers
float globalInput : register(C0) ; // access to Constant Float register
```

Global inputs are read-only within local functions, the same as global variables.

There are a number of register locations available in the GPU. Figure 7-2 shows the registers as related to the shader processor.

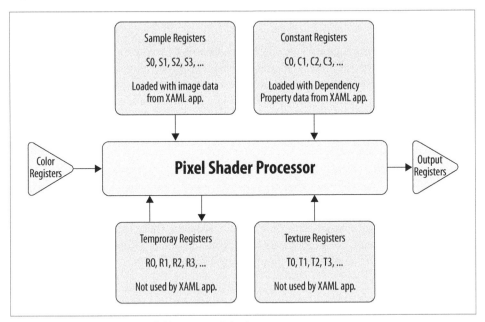

Figure 7-2. GPU registers available to a pixel shader

Not all the register groups offered by HLSL are available to XAML effects. The two areas exposed to your .NET code are the *Sampler* and *Constant* registers.

 Remember that the HLSL Global Constant registers are aliased to the .NET ShaderEffect dependency properties and the Sampler registers are filled with the Image values from the ShaderEffect.

Texture and Sampler Input

Both the texture register and sampler registers contain image information. To retrieve image information for use in your shader code, you'll use the Sampler registers. It's worth a short discussion of the two types of registers before continuing.

Learning which portions of the DirectX pixel shader architecture are not relevant to XAML effect development is crucial. Most of the documentation and resources assume you are creating 3D scenes. As such, they contain long discussions of textures, vertices, and other 3D concepts, which have little meaning in XAML effects.

The generic term for image data in DirectX is *texture*. Once again, the name depends on historical context and an understanding of 3D programming constructs. By themselves, 3D models are stark, geometrical representations of real-world objects. Texture mapping provides a means to add detailed surface texture to an otherwise bland monotone model.

Texture mapping is a process that takes image information and overlays it on the 3D model. For a real-world example, think back to the last time you gift wrapped a birthday present. The flat sheet of wrapping paper decorated with colorful symbols is analogous to the shader texture. The irregularly shaped container containing the gift is the model.

The texture registers, more properly called the *texture coordinate* registers, contain pointers to the actual texture data. For various reasons, these image handles are not what we need; instead, we need a way to sample the pixels available in the textures. For that reason, pixel shaders have Sampler registers.

Samplers are special read-only inputs intended to provide access to texture data. A texture in .NET shaders is usually the UI/Image data.

A sampler is bound to a texture. You can think of it as a wrapper around the texture, with some extra metadata and mapping that makes it possible to read pixel data from the texture.

Sampler Declarations

There are four types of textures in Direct3D, each with a different type name used in a sampler declaration. The image and UI textures passed in from your XAML effect are stored in 2D textures. Use the `sampler2D` type to declare samplers for the XAML input.

```
sampler2D a1 : register(S0); // Sampler register
```

Other texture declarations

The other samplers listed here are part of HLSL but are not readily usable in XAML. The problem is that there is no supported way to get the correct texture type passed from the XAML effect to the HLSL shader. I've added the samplers here for completeness.

1D textures are a 2D texture with the height clamped to one row. They are often used for color-map and gradient lookups. Declare with the `sampler` type.

3D textures, a.k.a. volume textures, contain several layers of 2D textures packed in a single structure. Declare with the `sampler3D` type.

A *cubemap texture* is a special structure containing six 2D textures. The six 2D textures are arranged in a cube pattern. Declare with the `samplerCUBE` type.

Other Code Constructs

HLSL supports the customary code constructs (expressions, statements, variables).

Flow Control—Branching

You probably use `if` statements and other branching keywords without much thought. After all, they have been part of the programming lexicon for decades. HLSL supports the usual suspects (`if, else, switch, break`). The syntax is familiar, identical to other C languages you may have seen.

While the syntax may be identical, there are philosophical differences to consider. These differences stem from two factors, the parallel nature of the GPU and the preferred GPU data type, the `float`.

The trouble with float

Here's a little secret about the HLSL-type system. Variables typed as `integer` and `Boolean` are subject to change, depending on the hardware available at runtime. The data type can be changed to a `float` in some circumstances.

What does that imply for the seemingly innocent code example shown in Example 7-31?

Example 7-31. If statement with int data type

```
[C#]
  int max = 5; // variable type might change to float in some conditions
  // other work here...
  if( max== 5 ){} ;
```

Developers with even a modicum of floating point experience know the trouble concealed in this code sample. A value stored in a float variable can experience rounding errors; the value in the max variable might be 4.9999999 or 5.0000001, instead the expected 5.0. That leaves a hole in our logic. It's a narrow gap, to be sure, but just the kind of breach a logic bug can sneak through.

The solution is not to test for equality with ==. Instead, use the <=, >= operators.

Parallel programming and branches

Pixel shaders run in parallel on the GPU, which means that your shader code is processed in batches, with hundreds of copies of the code running simultaneously. The GPU does everything in its power to ensure that each batch runs concurrently and that all the shaders finish near the same time. The bigger the batch, the faster the entire effect can proceed to completion.

Putting `if` and other branch statements in the code means that some items in the batch could finish many cycles later than their batch companions. This causes synchronization problems as batch items finish at different times. To prevent sync issues, the GPU analyzes the potential batch items and attempts to batch items with similar length logic sections.

Think about that for a minute. The more branch criteria, the more branch-specific batches are necessary. The more specific the batch, the fewer the number of pixel shaders that can be added to the batch. This reduces the GPU performance because it has to run more batches.

The newer PS_3_0 specification does a better job with branching performance. Unfortunately, Silverlight is stuck with the PS_2_0 specification.

Be aware that extensive branching might slow down the performance of your shader.

Flow Control—Loops

Repeating a section of code is easy. Use the looping keywords (`for`, `while`, `do`, `continue`). Though it may be easy, loops are troublesome on GPUs.

Consider a `for` loop that modifies ten items in an array. Many graphics cards don't actually support loops in a pixel shader, so the compiler just unrolls the `for` loop, forcing the shader to evaluate all ten iterations one after the other.

Loops suffer the same performance considerations mentioned in the branching section plus have additional quirks unique to their implementation. Use with caution.

> True flow control is only supported on hardware that meets PS_3_0 or newer specifications. For older hardware, the compiler converts the flow statements into inline code, unrolling loops and evaluating both sides of conditionals.

Operators

It's no surprise that HLSL contains operators. They are the bedrock of any programming language. Your favorite operator is probably available (see Table 7-5).

Table 7-5. Intrinsic Operators

++	--	&&	||	==	::
...	<<	>>	<<=	>>=	
<=	=>	*=	/=	+=	-=
!=	%=	&=	|=	^=	->
!	-	+	.	*	/
%	>	<	?:		

 Unlike other C languages, the ||, &&, and ?: expressions do not short-circuit. Both sides of the expression are always evaluated.

Most operators, including the comparison operators, work with the component name-space syntax. Consider the following (Example 7-32):

Example 7-32. Component namespace operators

```
float4 x = float4(0, .1, .2, .3);
x += .2; // x.r == .2, x.g == .3, x.b==.4, x.a==.5;
```

In Example 7-32, a single operator (+=) was used, yet the value of each item in the float4 vector was changed.

To use the comparison operators with vectors, employ the any() or all() intrinsic functions as shown in Example 7-33.

Example 7-33. Component namespace and comparison operators

```
float4 m = float4(.7, .7, .7, .7);

float4 a = float4(.5, .5, .5, .5);
float4 b = float4(.7, .5, .5, .5);
float4 c = float4(.7, .7, .7, .7);

if (any(a == m )){} // false
if (any(b == m )){} // true

if (all(b == m )){} // false
if (all(c == m )){} // true
```

Built-in Functions

HLSL comes with a set of intrinsic functions that provide access to most of the common algorithms necessary for shader work. You can find a list of all the intrinsic functions and some rudimentary documentation on the MSDN website at: *http://bit.ly/intrinsic functions*

Texture Functions

Sampling a pixel color from an input texture is a task that happens in nearly every shader. The texture functions provide the means to grab a color value from the sampler source.

By far, the most popular texture function for XAML shaders is text2D(). All the texture functions listed in Table 7-6 return a float4, which is the RGBA color sample at the specified texture coordinates.

Table 7-6. All the texture functions

tex1D	tex1Dbias	tex1Dgrad	tex1Dlod	tex1Dproj
tex2D	tex2Dbias	tex2Dgrad	tex2Dlod	tex2Dproj
tex3D	tex3Dbias	tex3Dgrad	tex3Dlod	tex3Dproj
tex4D	tex4Dbias	tex4Dgrad	tex4Dlod	tex4Dproj

Math Functions

The remainder of the built-in functions are classified as math functions (Tables 7-7 and 7-8.

Table 7-7. Trigonometry functions

sin	sinh	asin	
cos	cosh	acos	sincos
tan	tanh	atan	atan2

Table 7-8. Other math functions

abs	all	any	ceil	clamp	clip
cross	D3DCOLORtoUBYTE4	ddx	ddy	degrees	determinant
distance	dot	exp	exp2	faceforward	floor
fmod	frac	frexp	fwidth	isfinite	isinf
isnan	ldexp	/length	lerp	lit	log
log10	log2	max	min	modf	mul
noise	normalize	pow	radians	reflect	refract
round	rsqrt	saturate	sign	smoothstep	sqrt
step	transpose	trunc			

As you can see, there are about sixty math functions included in the API. Some of the functions are not usable from a pixel shader: for example, the random function only works at the vertex shader stage.

Useful Built-in Functions

I have my favorite intrinsic functions. Here are a few that I find useful for shader development. You'll find more examples in the next chapter.

Clamp and saturate

These functions are helpful for limiting the range of a value. The clamp function takes a minimum and maximum parameter. Saturate is identical to clamp, except the range values are hard coded to zero and one (Example 7-34).

Example 7-34. Clamp and saturate functions

```
float a = 7;
float result;
result = clamp(a, 2, 4); // min==2, max==4

// saturate clamps the value to the range 0 to 1
result = saturate(a);

// another example used in a calculation
float3 bloom = saturate((base - BloomThreshold) / (1 - BloomThreshold));
```

A typical use for the saturate function is during lighting calculations. Working with vectors and dot products, you can get negative values, using saturate clamps negative numbers to zero.

Lerp

I laugh every time I use this function. The funny sounding name is a shortened version of Linear Interpolation. I see this function in shaders everywhere. Linear interpolation is a simple formula for calculating values at positions in between the data points (Example 7-35).

Example 7-35. Lerp function

```
float4 black = float4(0,0,0,1);
float4 white = float4(1,1,1,1);
float4 gradient = lerp(black,white, uv.x );
```

This sample (Example 7-35) uses lerp to generate a grayscale gradient.

Summary

Your journey is nearly complete. This chapter showed the important HLSL language components, the building blocks of your shader code. Here you discovered the mechanics of the language, but that is only the first step to HLSL mastery.

The final segment in our HLSL tour is in the next chapter. There, you will learn how to use these programmatic elements to build your dream shaders.

CHAPTER 8

The Zen of Shader Programming

Zen of Pixel Programming

Now that you have the HLSL language concepts firmly in hand, let's consider how to use them in common scenarios. This final chapter explores the essential subjects that every shader developer needs to know.

Sampling a Pixel Color

Examine the main function signature in any shader code (Example 8-1).

Example 8-1. Sampling pixel color in shader

```
sampler2D input : register(S0);
float4 main(float2 uv : TEXCOORD) : COLOR
{

  float4 color;
  color= tex2D( input , uv.xy);

  return color;
}
```

The parameter passed into the function is typed as **float2**. It represents the x and y coordinates of the current pixel. As each pixel is processed by the shader, the **float2** parameter provides access to the current location. So what do you do with that information?

A common task is to use the coordinate to determine the current pixel color. To accomplish this task requires the talents of the **tex2D** function. I looked up the definition of the text2D function in the DirectX documentation and it states:

"Samples a 2D texture."

If the documentation writer was looking to accolades for the shortest answer, this little nugget is a prizewinner. Short, maybe, but not very useful. Let me try.

The `tex2D` function performs a texture lookup. In other words, it examines a given texture (a pointer to an image) and returns the color value at the specified location. There are other texture functions (`tex1D` and `tex3D`) available, but for now we'll stay with the 2D version. The 2D portion of the name stands for two-dimensional. Now, let's examine these two lines of code from the previous example (Example 8-2).

Example 8-2. Sampling the texture

```
float4 color;
color= tex2D( input , uv.xy);
```

The first parameter passed into `tex2D`, `input`, is the texture value to examine. The second parameter, `uv.xy`, represents the x, y coordinate to look up.

 Many shader examples show the uv parameter passed to the tex2D function with the swizzle syntax (**uv.xy**). This is not a requirement; using the uv variable unadorned with swizzles work just as well.

In this example, we are retrieving the color at the current pixel location. You can use any arbitrary x, y value though, which permits sampling other locations of the texture.

Once you have the color value stored in a `float4` variable, you can start modifying the value. Look at Example 8-1 again. What is that function doing with the color? Nothing. It is a pass-through shader; the color is unchanged by the HLSL code. The rest of this section shows how to modify the output color.

Sampling a Color from Another Texture

The color sample doesn't have to come from the main texture; we can get colors from other textures (Example 8-3).

Example 8-3. Sample a second texture

```
sampler2D input   : register(S0);
sampler2D another : register(S1);

float4 main(float2 uv : TEXCOORD) : COLOR
{
  // sample a pixel from another texture
  float4 color= tex2D( another , uv.xy);

  return color;
}
```

In Example 8-3, the pixel color of the original image is replaced with the pixel color from the second texture. For a subtler effect, let's try blending the colors from the two textures (Example 8-4).

Example 8-4. Blending two textures

```
// sample original texture
float4 original= tex2D( input , uv.xy);
// sample a pixel from another texture
float4 second= tex2D( another , uv.xy);

original.r =  original.r + second.b;
return original;
}
```

In Example 8-4, the red channel of the original texture is increased by the blue channel value in the second texture.

Colors

Pixel shaders excel at color manipulation. If you have an idea for a color-shifting algorithm, there are few barriers for realizing the desired outcome. The only limitation in building a fancy color shader lies in the limited number of instruction available in the PS_2_0 specification.

Complex shader algorithms often hit the maximum instruction count problem. Simply stated, targeting the PS_2_0 specification limits the instruction count to 64. The easiest solution, if you are a WPF developer, is to switch to the PS_3_0 spec, which gives you 400% more instructions. Silverlight developers cannot target PS_3_0.

Color Channel Manipulation

Changing the color levels in any of the RGBA channels is easy. Example 8-5 shows how to increase the blue channel by 30 percent.

Example 8-5. Increase blue channel

```
float4 outColor;
float4 color= tex2D( input , uv.xy);

// use the original red, green, and alpha value
outColor.rga= color.rga;
// increase the blue channel

// the blue channel is limited to values between 0.0 and 1.0
// calculated values higher than 1.0 are automatically clamped to 1.0
outColor.b = (color.b * 1.3);
return outColor;
```

Conditional Colors

Naturally, you can alter the color channel based on conditions. The next sample (Example 8-6) sets the pixel to either black or white depending on a threshold value.

Example 8-6. Black or white shader

```
sampler2D  InputTexture : register(S0);
///  <defaultValue>.6 </defaultValue>
float Threshold : register(C1);

float4 main(float2 uv : TEXCOORD) : COLOR
{
    float4 originalColor = tex2D(InputTexture, uv);
    float redValue = originalColor.r;
    float3 newColor;
    if (redValue < Threshold ){
      newColor = float3(0,0,0);}    // black
    else {
      newColor = float3(1,1,1);  } // white

    return float4(newColor, originalColor.a);
}
```

Preserving the alpha channel

There are times when you want to change the color of the pixel but leave the alpha channel (transparency level) at the original value. One interesting technique for doing this utilizes the `float4` constructor syntax (Example 8-7).

Example 8-7. Overloads of the float4 constructor

```
float   f1 = .2;
float2 f2 = .4;
float3 f3 = .6;
float4 f4 = .8;
float4 outColor;

// various overloads of the float4 constructor
outColor = float4(f1, f1, f1, f1); //r, g, b, a
outColor = float4(f2, f2);      //rb, ga
outColor = float4(f2, f1, f1); //rb, b, a
outColor = float4(f4,);      //rgba
outColor = float4(f3, f1); //rgb, a
```

Look at that last line in Example 8-7. It uses a `float3` and a `float` to create a `float4` value. The last argument maps to the alpha channel and that's the key to keeping the existing channel value (Example 8-8).

Example 8-8. Preserving the alpha channel

```
float4 originalColor = tex2D(InputTexture, uv);
float3  newColor = float3(1,1,1);  } // white

return float4(newColor, originalColor.a);
```

You can see an example of this technique in the Black and Whiter shader, shown in Example 8-6.

Replace a Color

For a more interesting effect, let's swap out one color for another. The code in Example 8-9 seeks out a color within a specified range and replaces it with another.

Example 8-9. Replace one color with another

```
sampler2D  InputTexture : register(S0);

///  <description>The target color to replace </description>
///  <defaultValue>Black</defaultValue>
float4 TargetColor : register(C0);

///  <description>The replacement color</description>
///  <defaultValue>White</defaultValue>
float4 ReplacementColor : register(C1);

///  <description>The tolerance</description>
///  <defaultValue>0.3</defaultValue>
float Tolerance  : register(C2);

float4 main(float2 uv : TEXCOORD) : COLOR
{
  float4 originalColor;
    originalColor = tex2D( InputTexture , uv.xy);
    if(originalColor.r < TargetColor.r + Tolerance
       && originalColor.r > TargetColor.r - Tolerance
       && originalColor.g < TargetColor.g + Tolerance
       && originalColor.g > TargetColor.g - Tolerance
       && originalColor.b < TargetColor.b + Tolerance
       && originalColor.b > TargetColor.b - Tolerance)
    {
    originalColor.rgb=ReplacementColor.rgb;
    }
    return float4(originalColor.rgb, originalColor.a);
}
```

Figure 8-1 shows the replace color effect applied to the flower image. Another example (see Figure 8-2) shows how to use the effect to replace the background color of an image.

Figure 8-1. Replace a color on a flower petal

Figure 8-2. Replace background color

Other Color Modifier Examples

Grayscale

The grayscale shader (Example 8-10) uses the intrinsic dot() function to change the colors to monotone. It also shows how add color tint to the grayscale. Figure 8-3 show the tint applied to a sample picture.

Example 8-10. Use dot function to create grayscale

```
float4 sourceColor = tex2D(input, uv);
float3 rgb = sourceColor.rgb;
```

```
 // use a popular grayscale weighting formula (0.30, 0.59, 0.11)
float3 luminance = dot(rgb, float3(0.30, 0.59, 0.11));
return float4(luminance , sourceColor.a);

// tint output with another color
float4 AnotherColor = float4(1, 0.85, 0.4, 1);
return float4(luminance * AnotherColor.rgb, sourceColor.a);
```

Figure 8-3. Grayscale with color tint

Cartoon shader

A cartoon shader takes the existing colors in an image and reduces the color fidelity. In some pictures, the resulting color banding looks similar to the reduced color palette seen in comic books. The key to making this shader work is the `floor()` function. The floor function takes a float parameter and returns the largest integer that is less than the specified value. It has a companion function named `ceil()` that takes a parameter and returns the largest integer greater than the incoming value (Example 8-11).

Example 8-11. Cartoon shader

```
float4 color = tex2D( input, uv );
color.rgb /= color.a;

int levels = 5;
color.rgb *= levels;        // increase all colors by factor
color.rgb = floor(color.rgb); // clip the color to the nearest integer value
color.rgb /= levels;        // decrease all colors by factor
color.rgb *= color.a;
return color;
}
```

Check out Figure 8-4 for an example of the cartoon shader in action.

Figure 8-4. Cartoon shader applied to flower image

Gloom shader

A gloom filter mimics a low-level lighting situation; for example, a murky deep woods vignette. Human eyesight in twilight conditions is a mixture of color and monochrome vision. To simulate this, a gloom shader desaturates the color spectrum, moving the colors toward the grayscale side. It also changes the contrast, accentuating the darker parts of the image (Example 8-12).

Example 8-12. A gloom shader

```
sampler2D inputSampler : register(S0);

/// <summary>Intensity of the gloom image.</summary>
/// <minValue>0</minValue>
/// <maxValue>1</maxValue>
/// <defaultValue>1</defaultValue>
float GloomIntensity : register(C0);
```

```
/// <summary>Intensity of the base image.</summary>
/// <minValue>0</minValue>
/// <maxValue>1</maxValue>
/// <defaultValue>0.5</defaultValue>
float BaseIntensity : register(C1);

/// <summary>Saturation of the gloom image.</summary>
/// <minValue>0</minValue>
/// <maxValue>1</maxValue>
/// <defaultValue>0.2</defaultValue>
float GloomSaturation : register(C2);

/// <summary>Saturation of the base image.</summary>
/// <minValue>0</minValue>
/// <maxValue>1</maxValue>
/// <defaultValue>1</defaultValue>
float BaseSaturation : register(C3);

float3 AdjustSaturation(float3 color, float saturation)
{
    // make graycale    float grey = dot(color, float3(0.3, 0.59, 0.11));
    // interoplate the gray and color values of the image

    return lerp(grey, color, saturation);
}

float4 main(float2 uv : TEXCOORD) : COLOR
{
    float GloomThreshold = 0.25;
    float4 color = tex2D(inputSampler, uv);
    float3 base = 1 - color.rgb / color.a;
    float3 gloom = saturate((base - GloomThreshold) / (1 - GloomThreshold));


    // Adjust color saturation and intensity.
    gloom = AdjustSaturation(gloom, GloomSaturation) * GloomIntensity;
    base = AdjustSaturation(base, BaseSaturation) * BaseIntensity;

    // Darken down the base image in areas where there is a lot of bloom,
    // to prevent things looking excessively burned-out.
    base *= (1 - saturate(gloom));

    // Combine the two images.
    return float4((1 - (base + gloom)) * color.a, color.a);
}
```

Figure 8-5 shows the cheerless results of the gloom filer.

The premultiplied alpha dilemma

Eventually you will create a color blending shader, combining pixel values from multiple inputs, and wonder what happened to your alpha channels. You've tripped over the premultiplied alpha implementation hidden within the XAML implementation. For

Figure 8-5. Gloom shader

performance reasons, the WPF team multiplies each color channel by the alpha channel before sending your input into the HLSL shader.

When you send your output back to XAML, you might need to premultiply the alpha channel (Example 8-13).

Example 8-13. Transparent colors and premultiply

```
sampler2D input : register(s0);


float4 main(float2 uv : TEXCOORD) : COLOR
{

  float4 purple= float4(1, 0, 1, 0);
  // purple will not be 100% transparent, as expected

  float4 yellow= float4(1, 1, 0, 0);
  pre-multiply alpha channel
  // before returning to XAML land
  yellow.rgb = yellow.rgb * yellow.a;
// yellow will be 100% transparent
  return yellow;
}
```

Coordinates

Finding a desired location in the input images is straightforward, at least if you remember that you are in a single-pixel function and are willing to abandon the absolute pixel position idea. Recall that the inbound parameter for the main shader function is the x, y location of the current pixel. The coordinates are normalized; you get a number between zero and one.

If you are working with the pixel at location (400,300) in an 800 × 600 image, the values are normalized as x==0.5 and y == 0.5 (Example 8-14).

Example 8-14. Normalized coordinates

```
float x = uv.x; // x == 0.5
float y = uv.y; // y == 0.5;
```

Because the input coordinate is normalized, working with other pixels in the same input texture is based on relative location to the current pixel. In most cases, this is acceptable.

If you truly need absolute positions for the pixel or want to know the texture size, you'll need to send the size value into shader code from outside the HLSL pipeline. The best solution for these circumstances is to add a size parameter to your XAML effect code (Example 8-15).

Example 8-15. Size parameter, as input constant to shader

```
// Mapped to XAML Dependency Property
// assign a size value in the XAML app before applying the effect
 float2 TextureSize : register(C0);
```

Drawing a vertical line

To show how the coordinates work, I'll draw a line in the HLSL code. This is achieved with an `if` statement that determines if the current pixel is in the center of the image. Since there are no shape primitives in HLSL, we are responsible for rendering the line output ourselves. Example 8-16 shows one way to draw a vertical line.

Example 8-16. Draw a white vertical line

```
sampler2D input : register(S0);

/// <summary>Left edge of line.</summary>
/// <minValue>0</minValue>
/// <maxValue>1.0</maxValue>
/// <defaultValue>.6</defaultValue>
float LeftEdge : register(C1);

float4 main(float2 uv : TEXCOORD) : COLOR {

  float4 color;
  float lineWidth = 0.003 ; // as a percent of total image size
  color= tex2D( input , uv.xy);

 if(uv.x > LeftEdge + lineWidth || uv.x < LeftEdge - lineWidth){
     // return the original color
     return color;
 }

  // otherwise, set the color to white
  return float4(1,1,1,1);
}
```

The next shader, Example 8-17, colors every other pixel column black. This code assumes that the original image size is passed into the shader through the input constant named SourceImageSize.

Example 8-17. Color alternate columns black

```
sampler2D input : register(S0);

/// <summary>The Size of the input texture.</summary>
float2 SourceImageSize : register(C0);

float4 main(float2 uv : TEXCOORD) : COLOR
{

  float4 color = float4(0,0,0,1); // black

  // find current postion based on source image size
  float horizontalPos = floor( uv.x * SourceImageSize.x) ;
  if((horizontalPos  % 2 ) >= 1    )
  {
    return tex2D(input, uv);
  }
  return color;
}
```

Pixelate

Learning how to draw lines is instructional; at least it's worthwhile when learning coordinates in HLSL. XAML already has the shape classes to handle these chores, however. It's better to use HLSL for pixel rendering tasks that are impossible to produce with normal XAML code. I've chosen the pixelate effect for our first look at these shader optimized tasks.

A *pixelate effect* simulates a closeup of an image (See Figure 8-6), causing it to appear coarser, blockier, and less detailed. The secret to this effect is how you sample the pixel value. Rather than sample each pixel, the shader code breaks the image in block-sized chunks. Only the center pixel of the block is sampled, after which the center color is applied to all pixels that fall within the block boundary (Example 8-18).

Example 8-18. Pixelate shader

```
/// <description>An effect that turns the input into blocky pixels.</description>

sampler2D input : register(S0);

/// <summary>The number of horizontal and vertical pixel blocks.
(6,4)== 6 columns, 4 rows</summary>
/// <type>Size</type>
/// <minValue>20,20</minValue>
/// <maxValue>100,100</maxValue>
/// <defaultValue>60,40</defaultValue>
float2 GridSize : register(C0);
```

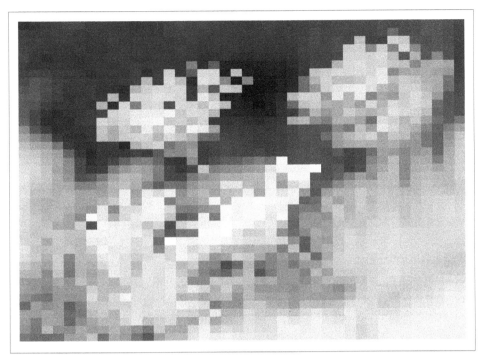

Figure 8-6. Pixelate shader

```
float4 main(float2 uv : TEXCOORD) : COLOR
{
    float4 color;
    float2 blockSizePercent = 1.0 / GridSize; // determine the block size

    // determine what cell contains current pixel
    float2 cellNum = floor(uv / blockSizePercent);
    // find the center of current block
    float2 centerOfBlock = (cellNum * blockSizePercent) + (blockSizePercent / 2);

    color = tex2D(input, centerOfBlock); // sample the center pixel of current block

    return color;
}
```

Convolution kernels

The pixelate example shows how to change the current pixel color based on the value of another nearby pixel. The shader world loves this idea and has a number of popular effects that use surrounding pixels. All the distortion effects are a variant of this concept.

Another popular category that uses this principle is the *convolution filter*. A convolution is an operation that calculates a pixel value based on the values of its neighbors. Rather than examining one neighbor, convolution filters rely on many neighbors to determine the final color of the current pixel.

Consider the pixel (uv) shown at the center of the 3×3 grid in Figure 8-7. It is surrounded by eight neighbors. Most pixels in a source image would fit into this grid, the only exceptions to this rule being the pixels near the edge of the image.

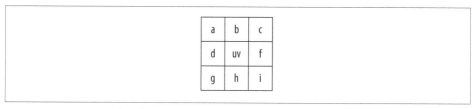

Figure 8-7. Current pixel and its neighbor pixels

Defining a weighting matrix

A convolution filter is based on a matrix lookup. Each cell in the matrix (3×3, 5×5, 7×7, etc.) contains a weight factor defining how much impact that neighbor pixel has on the final color output. Consider the 3×3 matrix shown in Figure 8-8.

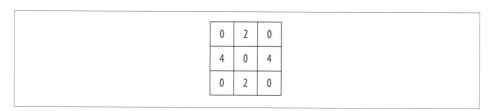

Figure 8-8. Convolution matrix with weight factors

The weighting factors indicated in Figure 8-8 are applied to the pixels shown in Figure 8-7 as follows.

(a*0)+(b*2)+(c*0)+(d*4)+(uv*0)+(f*4)+(g*0)+(h*2)+(i*0)

As you can see, the pixel colors at positions (b, d, f, and h) have the most influence on the revised pixel color.

There are many standard convolution matrix settings. They are often used as the basis of blur, sharpen, and edge detection effects. Figure 8-9 shows a 7×7 weighting matrix that approximates a Gaussian blur.

Building a convolution effect

Here's an approach to using convolution matrices in a shader. Add a float3x3 variable and populate it with the weighting values. Example 8-19 shows three different matrices; each one produces a different effect.

0	0	0	0	0	0	0
0	5	18	32	18	5	0
0	18	64	100	64	18	0
5	32	100	uv	100	32	5
0	18	64	100	64	18	0
0	5	18	32	18	5	0
0	0	0	0	0	0	0

Figure 8-9. Gaussian Blur matrix

Example 8-19. Three convolution matrices in HLSL

```
// emboss convolution matrix
float3x3 filter = {-2.0,-1.0, 0.0,  // row 1
                   -1.0, 1.0, 1.0,  // row 2
                    0.0, 1.0, 2.0   // row 3
                  };
// 45 degree edge detect convolution matrix
float3x3 filterb = {-1, 2, -1,  // row 1
                    -1, 2, -1,  // row 2
                    -1, 2, -1   // row 3
                   };
// box blur convolution matrix
float3x3 filterc = {.1, .1, .2,  // row 1
                    .1, .1, .1,  // row 2
                    .1, .1, .1   // row 3
                   };
```

The next step is to get the neighbor pixels and load them into a `float3x3` variable (Example 8-20). To get the pixel granularity needed, use the technique shown earlier where the image size is passed into the shader as an input constant (`textureSize`).

Example 8-20. GetNeighborPixel helper function

```
float4 GetNeighborPixel(float2 uv,  float2 pixelOffset)
{
  //size of one pixel based on original image size;
  float pixelSize =  1.0f / textureSize ;
  return tex2D (input, uv ı pixelSize * pixelOffset);
}
```

Finally, the convolution matrix values and neighbor pixel values are combined (multiplied and totaled), then mixed with the original image colors (Example 8-21).

Example 8-21. The complete edge detect convolution effect

```
sampler2D input : register(S0);

/// <summary>Original images size.</summary>
/// <minValue>0,0/minValue>
/// <maxValue>800,800</maxValue>
/// <defaultValue>550,350</defaultValue>
float2 textureSize :register(C1);

/// <summary>Strength of effect mixed with original image.</summary>
/// <minValue>0/minValue>
/// <maxValue>1</maxValue>
/// <defaultValue>.6 </defaultValue>
float Strength : register(C0);

float4 GetNeighborPixel(float2 uv,  float2 pixelOffset)
{
  //size of one pixel based on original image size;
  float pixelSize =  1.0f / textureSize ;
  return tex2D (input, uv + (pixelSize  * pixelOffset));
}
float4 main(float2 uv : TEXCOORD) : COLOR
{
  // 45 degree edge detect convolution matrix
  float3x3 filter = {-1, 2, -1, // row 1
                     -1, 2, -1,  // row 2
                     -1, 2, -1  // row 3
                     };
  float3x3 currentPixels;
  currentPixels._11 = GetNeighborPixel(uv ,float2(-1,-1));
  currentPixels._21 = GetNeighborPixel(uv ,float2(-1, 0));
  currentPixels._31 = GetNeighborPixel(uv ,float2(-1, 1));

  currentPixels._12 = GetNeighborPixel(uv ,float2(0,-1));
  currentPixels._22 = GetNeighborPixel(uv ,float2(0, 0));
  currentPixels._32 = GetNeighborPixel(uv ,float2(0, 1));

  currentPixels._13 = GetNeighborPixel(uv ,float2(1,-1));
  currentPixels._23 = GetNeighborPixel(uv ,float2(1, 0));
  currentPixels._33 = GetNeighborPixel(uv ,float2(1, 1));

  float4 convo = filter._11*currentPixels._11 +
                 filter._21*currentPixels._21 +
                 filter._31*currentPixels._31 +
                 filter._12*currentPixels._12 +
                 filter._22*currentPixels._22 +
                 filter._32*currentPixels._32 +
                 filter._13*currentPixels._13 +
                 filter._23*currentPixels._23 +
                 filter._33*currentPixels._33 ;

  return lerp(float4(convo.rgb ,1),tex2D (input, uv) , Strength);
}
```

It's hard to see the results of the edge detect shader in Figure 8-10 as the effect is subtle. If you look closely at the petal flowers, especially in the center of the image, you can see a lightening of the top edges.

Figure 8-10. Edge detect applied to image

Distortion and Displacement Effects

The distortion effects are some of the zaniest effects seen in the shader pantheon. All the effects in this category rely on moving existing pixels within the image to new locations.

Here is a simple effect (Example 8-22) that copies the pixels on the right side of the source to the left side of the output (see Figure 8-11 for results).

Example 8-22. Copy and move pixels

```
sampler2D input : register(S0);

float4 main(float2 uv : TEXCOORD) : COLOR
{

  float4 Color;

 // determine if pixel is on left half of texture
 if(uv.x < 0.5 ){
   // get the color from the pixel located 50% to the right of current pixel
   return tex2D(input, float2(uv.x + 0.5, uv.y )) ;
 }
  Color= tex2D( input , uv.xy);
  return Color;
}
```

Figure 8-11. Copy right side pixels to left side of image

The next effect (Example 8-23) copies the values from an adjacent pixel and adds to the current color value. This creates an offset or echo copy of the image. The code in Example 8-23 creates one copy of the image. Try increasing the CopyCount value to see a blurrier output.

Example 8-23. Blur effect by copying pixel values

```
sampler2D  input : register(S0);

/// <summary>The center of the blur.</summary>
/// <minValue>0,0</minValue>
/// <maxValue>1,1</maxValue>
/// <defaultValue>0.9,0.6</defaultValue>
float2 Offset : register(C0);

/// <summary>The amount of blur.</summary>
/// <minValue>0</minValue>
/// <maxValue>0.2</maxValue>
/// <defaultValue>0.1</defaultValue>
float ScaleFactor : register(C1);

float4 main(float2 uv : TEXCOORD) : COLOR
{
 // float2 center = float2(.9,.6);
  const float CopyCount = 2;
```

```
  float4 color = 0;
  uv -= Offset;

  for (int i = 0; i < (CopyCount ); i++)  {
    float scale = 1.0 + ScaleFactor * (i / CopyCount);
    // sample the pixel from adjacent location, and add to existing color value
    color += tex2D(input, uv * scale + Offset);
  }

  color /= CopyCount;
  return color;
}
```

Figure 8-12 shows the blur copy effect applied to a checkerboard pattern.

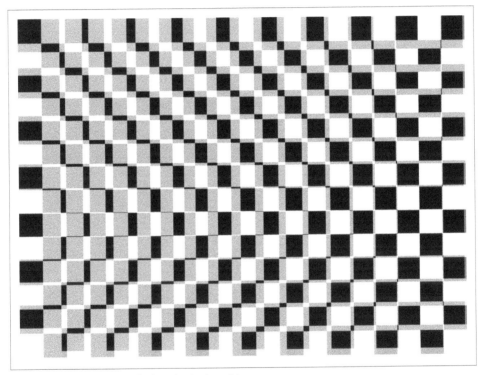

Figure 8-12. Blur copy applied to checkerboard image

For a curvier distortion effect, turn to the trigonometry functions. Using the cosine function, as demonstrated in Example 8-24, results in the S shaped distortion shown in Figure 8-13.

Example 8-24. Using the Cosine function

```
sampler2D input : register(S0);

/// <summary>Intensity of the Cosine value</summary>
```

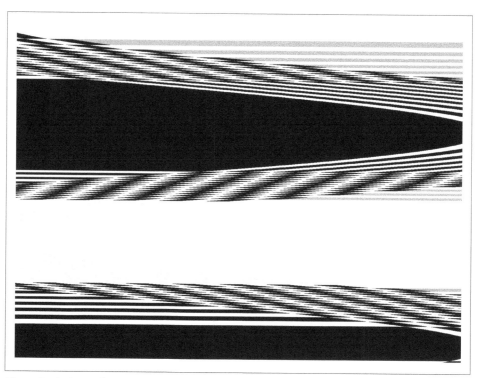

Figure 8-13. Cosine function applied to checkerboard image

```
/// <minValue>0/minValue>
/// <maxValue>100</maxValue>
/// <defaultValue>3</defaultValue>
float ratio : register(C0);
float4 main(float2 uv : TEXCOORD) : COLOR
{
  float2 offset = cos( uv.y * ratio );

  // use the offset value to sample another pixel
  float4  color= tex2D(input, uv + offset  );

  return color;
}
```

For the final distortion example, let's recreate the ubiquitous ripple effect (see Example 8-25).

Example 8-25. The Ripple shader

```
sampler2D input : register(S0);

/// <summary>The amplitude of the ripples.</summary>
/// <minValue>0</minValue>
/// <maxValue>1</maxValue>
/// <defaultValue>0.1</defaultValue>
float Amplitude : register(C1);

/// <summary>The frequency of the ripples.</summary>
/// <minValue>0</minValue>
/// <maxValue>100</maxValue>
/// <defaultValue>70</defaultValue>
float Frequency: register(C2);

float4 main(float2 uv : TEXCOORD) : COLOR
{
  float2 center = {0.5,0.5};
  float2 centerVector = uv - center; // vector from center to pixel
  centerVector.y /= 1.5; //set aspect ratio
  float dist = length(centerVector);
  centerVector /= dist;


  float2 wave;
  // the last two parameters to the sincos function
  // are output parameters
  // the function loads one with the sin value
  // and the other with the cosine value
  sincos(Frequency * dist , wave.x, wave.y);

  float falloff = 1 - dist;
  falloff *= falloff;

  dist += Amplitude * wave.x * falloff;
  float2 otherPoint = center + dist * centerVector;
  // sample the other point
  float4 color = tex2D(input, otherPoint);

  return color;
}
```

No wonder this is a popular effect. Look at the beautiful patterns created (see Figure 8-14) when the ripple effect is applied to a checkerboard image.

Figure 8-14. Ripple effect applied to checkerboard

Random Values

Most programming languages have a random number generator. HLSL has one, but it only works with vertex shaders. You can write your own pseudo-random generator using irrational numbers (Example 8-26).

Example 8-26. Pseudo-random number generator

```
float Random( float seed )
{
  // returns a number between 0 and 1
  const float pi = 3.1415926;
  return frac(tan(fmod(212121212,  1000 * seed * pi ) ) );
}
```

To demonstrate this function, I'll write a shader that draws random vertical white lines on the output. This is a favorite technique when creating old movie simulations, the lines mimicking the film scratches seen on timeworn film stock (Example 8-27).

Example 8-27. Use random function to draw white lines

```
sampler2D input : register(S0);

/// <summary>The value that triggers the scratch visibility</summary>
/// <minValue>0.9</minValue>
/// <maxValue>1</maxValue>
/// <defaultValue>.99</defaultValue>
float Threshold : register(C0);

/// <summary>The seed value to use for random function</summary>
/// <minValue>0</minValue>
/// <maxValue>1</maxValue>
/// <defaultValue>0</defaultValue>
float RandomSeed : register(C1);

float Random( float seed )
{
  // returns a number between 0 and 1
  const float pi = 3.1415926;
  return frac(tan(fmod(212121212,  1000 * seed * pi ) ) );
}

float4 main(float2 uv : TEXCOORD) : COLOR
{

  float4 color;

  color= tex2D(input , uv.xy);
  // seed the random function with x location and seed value
  float resultX = Random(uv.x + RandomSeed);

  if(resultX > Threshold)
  {
  color.rgb = 1;
  }

  return color;
}
```

All the caveats about random number generators apply; in particular, given the same seed number, this generator will always return the same "random" number.

Figure 8-15 shows the random lines created by this shader.

Figure 8-15. Image with random lines

Using a custom random generator function consumes instruction slots. When compiling to a PS_2_0 shader, this may be a concern. If so, there is another approach often used in shaders, namely sampling a noise lookup texture.

Another possibility is to calculate the random number in the .NET code and pass it as a parameter from the XAML effect.

Noise Textures

In many scenarios, a texture lookup provides a more satisfying approach to randomness than a computer algorithm. For these types of lookups, the source image is a pregenerated, random texture map. In game programming terminology, a distinction is often made between noise and static texture maps. In both cases, the pixels are computer-generated into a bitmap using well-known noise generation techniques. The differences between the two can be seen in Figure 8-16.

A static texture map is an image with randomly distributed color points. There is no discernible relationship between an individual pixel and its neighbors. Examine a group of pixels in Figure 8-16.a. There is clustering of groups of black and white pixels, but the transitions between neighbor pixels are jagged and disconnected.

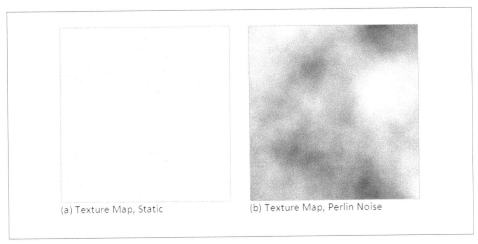

(a) Texture Map, Static   (b) Texture Map, Perlin Noise

Figure 8-16. Static and noise texture maps.

In a noise map, the value of each pixel changes smoothly as you transition between neighbor pixels (Figure 8-16.b). Noise maps, while randomly regenerated, produce more natural-looking bitmaps. This makes them indispensable for naturalizing 3D rendering output, where they are often used for terrain mapping, cloud generation, and natural material enhancements (wood, marble, etc.).

Creating static texture map

Any commercial photo editor, such as Adobe Photoshop or GIMP, has noise generation tools. Here's how to use the noise feature in Paint.NET to create a static texture map.

First, choose the Add Noise command from the Effect menu (shown in Figure 8-17).

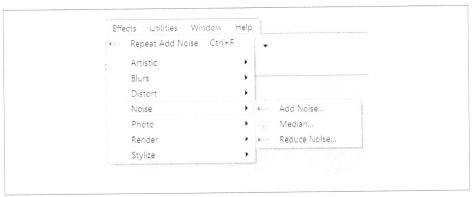

Figure 8-17. The Paint.NET Noise menu

In the Add Noise dialog, change the distribution sliders to preview the generated image. Figure 8-18 shows the settings that generate a sparse distribution of colored pixels.

Figure 8-18. Add noise dialog with sparse settings

Figure 8-19 shows the settings that generate a dense grayscale distribution.

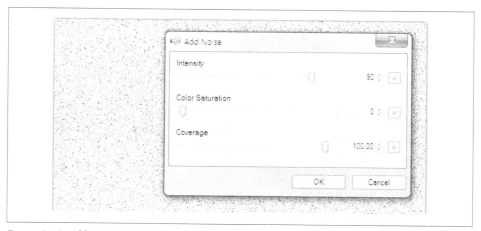

Figure 8-19. Add noise dialog with dense settings

Sampling the static map

To access the random pixel values, create a multi-input shader and use the static map as an additional input sampler to the effect.

The shader shown in Example 8-28 uses the pixel color from the static map to determine whether to draw a white line.

Example 8-28. Draw lines based on texture lookup

```
sampler2D input : register(S0);
sampler2D noiseSample : register(S1);

/// <summary>The grayscale value that triggers the scratch visibility</summary>
/// <minValue>0/minValue>
/// <maxValue>1</maxValue>
/// <defaultValue>.5</defaultValue>
float GrayScaleThreshold : register(C0);

/// <summary>What seed value to use for noise lookup (row)</summary>
/// <minValue>0/minValue>
/// <maxValue>1</maxValue>
/// <defaultValue>0</defaultValue>
float NoiseSeed : register(C2);


float4 main(float2 uv : TEXCOORD) : COLOR
{

  float3 randomColor = tex2D(noiseSample, float2(uv.x, NoiseSeed));
  float4 color = tex2D(input , uv.xy);

 // if all the rgb channels in the random pixel
 // are greater than the threshold value
  if(all(randomColor > GrayScaleThreshold)  )
  {
    color.rgb = 1; // set the color to white
  }

  return color; // otherwise, return the original color
}
```

Perlin Noise in Shaders

Back in the predawn era of 3D programming, texture mapping was the go-to method for making 3D objects look realistic. But texture mapping had problems of its own. For one, the textures often displayed repeated patterns that destroyed the illusion of reality. A small group of graphics pioneers determined that applying a noise generator to the texture map solved the problem.

Noise, as we've seen earlier, is a random set of pixels with special attributes. The trick in creating noise samples is generating the random points while forcing a smooth transition between the neighboring points. Ken Perlin, professor at New York University, is famous for writing an algorithm in the 1980s that accomplishes this mission in a fast and practical manner. His technique lives on and is still utilized in shader development today.

The Perlin function is useful for creating dynamic noise, but it consumes many shader instruction slots. The Simplex noise function is a newer and leaner noise generator.

To work with Perlin noise, write an HLSL function that generates the noise values or create a Perlin noise map with a photo-editing tool and sample the noise values. Without a doubt, the simplest approach is to use a photo-editing tool to generate a Perlin noise bitmap.

In Paint.NET, this feature is hidden in the Effects→Render→Clouds menu (Figure 8-20).

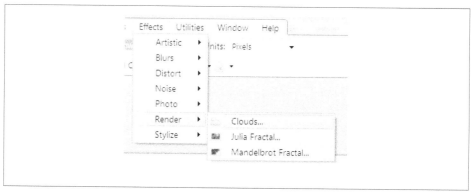

Figure 8-20. Generate a noise bitmap with the clouds menu

Figure 8-21 shows the settings that generate a high-contrast noise bitmap.

According to the HLSL documentation, there is an intrinsic `noise()` function. Don't waste your time researching the function, as it is not available in pixel shaders.

Noise lookup in a distortion shader

As you've seen, we can use the trigonometry functions to distort the output into interesting shapes. Noise maps can also be used as distortion influences and provide complex curves that are hard to attain with traditional trig functions.

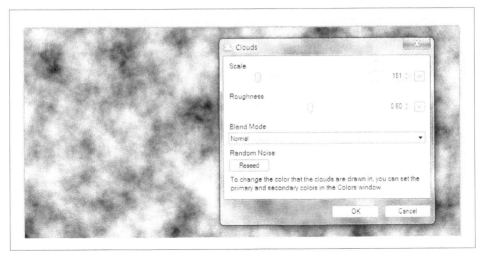

Figure 8-21. Use the Clouds tool in Paint.NET

For the next two shader examples, I'm using a noise map (see Figure 8-22) created in Paint.Net.

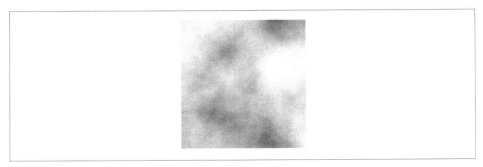

Figure 8-22. Noise map used in the examples

In the first shader (Example 8-29), I'm creating an effect that simulates rippling cloth (see Figure 8-23). Rather than sample the entire noise map, I'll use a single row of pixels obtained with this code snippet.

```
tex2D( noiseInput , float2(uv.x, NoiseSeed));
```

Example 8-29. Distortion effect with noise map sampling

```
sampler2D input : register(S0);
sampler2D noiseInput : register(S1);

/// <summary>Chooses a single row from the noise map</summary>
/// <minValue>0</minValue>
/// <maxValue>1</maxValue>
/// <defaultValue>0</defaultValue>
```

Figure 8-23. Cloth ripple effect

```
float NoiseSeed : register(C0);

/// <summary>Change the size of the output.</summary>
/// <minValue>-1</minValue>
/// <maxValue>1</maxValue>
/// <defaultValue>.1</defaultValue>
float Size : register(C1);

float4 main(float2 uv : TEXCOORD) : COLOR
{
  float4 samplePoint = tex2D( noiseInput , float2(uv.x, NoiseSeed));

  // use the red channel to nudge the current pixel
  float4 color = tex2D( input , saturate( uv + samplePoint.r * Size));

  return color ;
}
```

This effect is especially satisfying when an animation is applied to the `NoiseSeed` parameter.

Noise lookup in a lighting shader

A pleasant dappled lighting effect is possible using noise maps. The shader in Example 8-30 modifies the colors of the image based on the noise map, which simulates light reflecting off a sunlit pool onto the image (See Figure 8-24).

Example 8-30. Dappled light effect

```
sampler2D input : register(S0);
sampler2D noiseInput : register(S1);

/// <summary>Chooses a single row from the noise map</summary>
/// <minValue>0</minValue>
/// <maxValue>1</maxValue>
/// <defaultValue>0</defaultValue>
float NoiseSeed : register(C0);

/// <summary>Ratio of noise to orignal image</summary>
/// <minValue>-1</minValue>
/// <maxValue>1</maxValue>
/// <defaultValue>.1</defaultValue>
float Ratio : register(C1);

float4 main(float2 uv : TEXCOORD) : COLOR
{

    float4 samplePoint = tex2D( noiseInput , float2(uv.x, NoiseSeed));

    float4 color = tex2D( input ,uv);
    // use the noise map to create highlights in output (dappled light)
    color = float4(lerp(samplePoint.rgb, color.rgb, Ratio), color.a);
    return color;
}
```

 For a fascinating look at real-time Perlin noise, try René Schulte's Silverlight sample. *http://bit.ly/PerlinSilverlight*

Summary

I vividly recall my early infatuation with drawing and animating items on an antiquated Apple IIGS computer. At that early point in time, with my limited programming skills, I struggled just to make a single red pixel move across the screen. But I was entranced, beguiled by the thought of making the visions I saw in my head a reality on that tiny cathode-lit screen.

I'm still chasing those visions today, albeit with hardware and software that is immensely more powerful than what was available on that old computer. My wildest graphics dreams on that long ago winter day are now a reality on my smartphone.

Figure 8-24. Dappled effect applied to checkerboard image

The rapid advances in the desktop computer industry are a boon to the 3D programming community, too. DirectX and HLSL give you the power to create effects that until recently were only achievable on the server farms of the movie industry elite.

These once-exclusive tools are now in your hands. Go out and make awesome effects. I can't wait to see what you will build with XAML and HLSL.

Resources

Books

- Reed: Learning XNA 4.0 (*http://oreil.ly/Lbkixf*)
- Brown: Silverlight 5 in Action (*http://manning.com/pbrown/*)
- Bugnion: Silverlight 4 Unleashed (*http://amzn.to/LbkGfd*)

Programming

- NVidia Developer Zone (*http://developer.nvidia.com/resources*)

Premultiplied Alpha Blending

- Shawn Hargreaves (*http://bit.ly/Lbm01u*)

Convolution

- Convolution theory (*http://bit.ly/LZDu6a*)

Noise

- Noise in shaders (*http://bit.ly/KBtjkl*)
- Ken Perlin's NYU page (*http://mrl.nyu.edu/~perlin/*)

Tools

- Shazzam Shader Editor (*http://shazzam-tool.com*)
- ATI RenderMonkey (*http://bit.ly/LbmUen*)
- NVidia FX Composer (*http://developer.nvidia.com/fx-composer*)
- Visual Studio 11 (*http://www.microsoft.com/visualstudio/*)

Shazzam Settings

Table B-1. Shazzam tags, general and class level

Shazzam Tag	Description
///	A Shazzam XML comment tag. Content is ignored by the DirectX compiler.
<class>	Specifies the desired classname for generated file. By default, Shazzam uses the filename for the effect name. A class named SwirlyEffect is generated from the Swirly.fx file. Use the <class> tag to override the default name.
<namespace>	Specifies the desired namespace for the effect class. By default, Shazzam uses the namespace configured in the Tools panel settings panel. Use the <namespace> tag to override the default namespace name.
<description>	Provides a description for this effect. Shazzam will generate comments in the .cs/.vb file from this description.
<target>	Forces the compiler to generate a Silverlight or WPF version of the .NET effect class. The default target is configured in the Settings panel. Use the <target> tag to override the default target.
<type>	Use the <type> tag to change the default .NET type specified for the generated dependency property.

Table B-2. Shazzam Tags, parameter level

Shazzam Tag	Description
<summary>	This tag is used by the Tryout tab.
	It is used on a shader input parameter to describe the purpose of the input parameter. It causes a tooltip to show in Shazzam for the test control.
<minValue>	This tag is used by the Tryout tab.
	It provides an initial value for the minimum textbox.
<maxValue>	This tag is used by the Tryout tab.
	It provides an initial value for the maximum textbox.
<defaultValue>	This tag is used by the Tryout tab.
	It provides a starting value for the value slider.

About the Author

Walt's enthusiasm for crafting software interfaces blossomed early. Just a few days after discovering how to make pixels move around the screen of a borrowed computer, he was devouring books on the topic of computer graphics and UI design. Now he travels the world, speaking at software conferences and teaching a diverse portfolio of programming topics for corporate clients. On the consulting side, he continues to work with customers like Microsoft, HP, Intel, and Intuit and enjoys being part of the Wintellect consultant group. Recently, he has entered the video training market producing .NET titles for Lynda.com He writes for several publications including Code Magazine and TechTarget.com. His current UI obsession revolves around the Windows 8 Metro, Silverlight, Surface, and WPF APIs. You can find his blog at blog.wpfwonderland.com. Walt is also a Microsoft MVP and author of the free Shazzam WPF Shader utility (*http://shazzam-tool.com*).

Get even more for your money.

Join the O'Reilly Community, and register the O'Reilly books you own. It's free, and you'll get:

- $4.99 ebook upgrade offer
- 40% upgrade offer on O'Reilly print books
- Membership discounts on books and events
- Free lifetime updates to ebooks and videos
- Multiple ebook formats, DRM FREE
- Participation in the O'Reilly community
- Newsletters
- Account management
- 100% Satisfaction Guarantee

Signing up is easy:

1. **Go to: oreilly.com/go/register**
2. **Create an O'Reilly login.**
3. **Provide your address.**
4. **Register your books.**

Note: English-language books only

To order books online:
oreilly.com/store

For questions about products or an order:
orders@oreilly.com

To sign up to get topic-specific email announcements and/or news about upcoming books, conferences, special offers, and new technologies:
elists@oreilly.com

For technical questions about book content:
booktech@oreilly.com

To submit new book proposals to our editors:
proposals@oreilly.com

O'Reilly books are available in multiple DRM-free ebook formats. For more information:
oreilly.com/ebooks

Lightning Source UK Ltd.
Milton Keynes UK
UKHW031047170521
383862UK00006B/282

9 781449 319847